HOW.

Music, Metamorphosis and Capitalism

Music, Metamorphosis and Capitalism
Self, Poetics and Politics

Edited by

John Wall

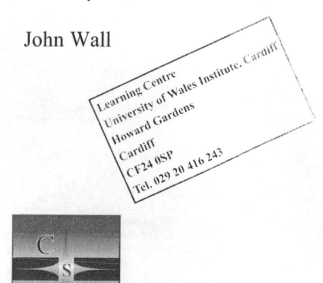

Learning Centre
University of Wales Institute, Cardiff
Howard Gardens
Cardiff
CF24 0SP
Tel. 029 20 416 243

CAMBRIDGE SCHOLARS PUBLISHING

Music, Metamorphosis and Capitalism: Self, Poetics and Politics, edited by John Wall

This book first published 2007 by

Cambridge Scholars Publishing

15 Angerton Gardens, Newcastle, NE5 2JA, UK

British Library Cataloguing in Publication Data
A catalogue record for this book is available from the British Library

ISBN 1-84718-133-3; ISBN 13: 9781847181336

Dedicated to my brother, Michael Wall, and friend, Patrick O'Mahony, both of whom have exercised a profound influence on my existential and intellectual orientation to music: my brother—the socio-psychological composition of the lyric: my friend—the intellectual necessity of the aesthetic.

Directly, in itself, music signifies nothing, unless by convention or association. Music means nothing and yet means everything.
Vladimir Jankélévitch, *Music and the Ineffable*

TABLE OF CONTENTS

LIST OF ILLUSTRATIONS

ACKNOWLEDGEMENTS

These papers came together over time through a number of gatherings, the seminal event being the Inscriptions in the Sand conference series held in Northern Cyprus, the last one taking place in 2005. Various forums in cyberspace and (now defunct) local cafés followed, until eventually this collection took shape. I would like to express my appreciation to all who contributed to these gatherings especially Rodney Sharkey, who, with seemingly inexhaustible reserves of energy, drove these events, instigating debate and offering novel solutions where conventional academic discourse foundered. Suzie Mirghani enriched this environment with her will to power, deflating hermeneutic positions in order to test her own strategic hypotheses. During the period this project was in gestation I attended regularly the concerts of guitarist, Matthew Gould and violinist, Beth Ilana Schneider, whose music sustained not only my sanity but the desire to engage in musical discourse, of both an aesthetic and sociological nature. For his insights into the compositional techniques of "found art" I owe a debt of gratitude to composer and photographer Shane Fage. For their technical assistance, let me express my thanks to Mahboubeh Abbaszadeh, Ahmet Gildir and Amir Hossein Khonsari. Finally, I would like to express my amazement and gratitude to Mahboubeh Abbaszadeh for the constancy of her belief in the validity of the imaginative life.

INTRODUCTION

> At the still point of the turning world. Neither flesh nor fleshless;
> Neither from nor towards; at the still point, there the dance is,
> But neither arrest nor movement. And do not call it fixity...[1]

I

One may suppose that normally, at least according to a reconstructive logic, it is the promising nature of a complex problematic, rich hermeneutic possibilities, barely glimpsed pathways and tantalizing conclusions that lead to the publishing of the results of intellectual activity. In this instance, however, it was a kind of unease or anxiety over difficulties inherent in aesthetic discourse that prompted me to set up this project.

The turning of academic attention to popular culture, especially popular music has been a project of immense liberation. The artificial and pretentious discourse that claimed only classical and / or traditional ethnic music was rich enough in content and structure to warrant musicological or anthropological attention has been laid to rest. It has been shown to be spuriously ideological in so far as it appropriated exclusively to itself the term "music", when in fact it was an expression of certain norms and aspirations to power of a complacent middle class.

The decks being cleared though, there is a distinct anxiety about discussing the aesthetics of music, whether it is "contemporary music" composed by those trained in the classical tradition or popular music written by those who tend to learn "orally", from the recordings of others. Composers like Pierre Boulez, John Cage and Morton Feldman tend to discuss the aesthetics of contemporary music as a rejection of earlier historical forms. Arch grump, Theodor Adorno is probably the most trenchant of all modernist writers in his demand that music take on a new rigour in its emphatic rejection of the accreted and false aesthetics of the classical music tradition: "Today the only works which really count are those which are no longer works at all."[2] And a composer as radical as Yiannis Xenakis speaks endlessly and fascinatingly about stochastic clusters and the Pythagorean provenance of his music, without ever offering a word on aesthetics, as if the sole value of music lay in the fact of its derivation from a set

---

[1] T. S. Eliot, *Four Quartets* (London: Faber and Faber, 1979) 5.
[2] Theodor Adorno, *Philosophy of Modern Music,* 30.

of operations and mathematically random mutations. Pythagoras of course built a monastic order around the aesthetics of his *musica mundana*, a music so rarified that it eschewed anything as crudely material as sound. Indeed, it is this association of aesthetics with cult (or class) belief that haunted the twentieth century and blocked the discussion of aesthetics. Certainly with Adorno this seems to have been the case:

> Advanced music has no recourse but to insist upon its own ossification without concession to that would-be humanitarianism which it sees through, in all its attractive and alluring guises, as the mask of inhumanity.[3]

Here, Adorno expresses a profound and, as it has turned out, enduring mistrust of a socially fixed idea of taste that insists on its universal application as an arbitrator of what constitutes acceptable and unacceptable music. For Adorno, the "mask of inhumanity" is not just some kind of historic misjudgement. It is a lethal delusion that reveals itself as the cruel presumption serving the venal self interest of an ascendant social class. The same mistrust of the aesthetic characterizes attitudes towards popular music. Simon Frith notes that popular culture studies have generally come to accept the appreciation of music as an act of consumption, performatively rebuffing Adorno's anxiety over the demeaning role of the culture industry in standardising musical absorption. In so doing, however, perhaps reflexively, aesthetic considerations are eliminated from the conceptualisation of the cultural value of such music and replaced by notions of strategic consumption, resistance and empowerment. Thus, there is a correct way to consume, a conclusion Frith is far from content with:

> Cultural value is assessed according to measures of true and false consciousness; aesthetic issues, the politics of excitement, say, or grace, are subordinated to the necessities of ideological interpretation, the call for 'demystification'"[4]

Frith suggests here that the study of popular music stands to learn a great deal about aesthetics from the more open aesthetic debates that occur in philosophy and literature, confident that popular culture studies have nothing to fear. However, it would be naïve to suppose that redress of the aesthetic deficit might be brought about with reference to other fields less harried by politics. Just as was the case in Adorno's thought, a cursory glance at philosophy and literary theory reveals a general mistrust of aesthetics. Terry Eagleton, in his usual chiding style, dismisses the Kantian project as an exercise in ideology:

---

[3] Theodor Adorno, *Ibid,* 20.
[4] Simon Frith, "Defending Popular Culture from the Populists", 104.

> The Kantian subject of aesthetic judgement, who misperceives as a quality of the object what is in fact a pleasurable coordination of its own powers, and who constitutes in a mechanistic world a figure of idealized unity, resembles the infantile narcissist of the Lacanian mirror stage, whose misperceptions Louis Althusser has taught us to regard as an indispensable structure of all ideology."[5]

The aesthetic in Kant was seen as a kind of knowledge, one that would bridge the gap between sense perception and categorical knowledge, thus bringing about the unity of the subject of knowledge.[6] It is the devolution of the unity of experience onto the abstract representation of the subject that Eagleton finds most objectionable in this formulation. This critical position is to be found in thinkers like Adorno, who is scathing about the "arrogance of the aesthetic subject, which says "we," while in reality it is still only "I."[7] Composers like John Cage also sought to rid their aesthetics of any residue of the subject as a central, all-knowing, organizing principle.[8] Furthermore, aesthetic judgement in Kant derives its rationality from the moral subject, without any consciousness on the part of Kant, that this self-regarding subject is conditioned in its ethical being by the norms of a historically specific culture and social class. It is ultimately the reduction of the Apollonian dimension of aesthetics to the moral subject that prompts accusations of narcissism and arrogance.

A writer on music like Simon Frith is then to be commended for his tenacity in entering this mine field. However, there is an element in Kantian aesthetics that may be drawn upon to circumvent, for the time being, the thorny problems of aesthetic judgement. In a telling phrase that combines both redemptive and damning qualities, Kant expresses the salient points of his aesthetic philosophy:

> The aesthetic judgement … refers the representation, by which an Object is given, solely to the Subject and brings to our notice no quality of the object, but only *the final form in the determination of the powers of representation engaged upon it.*[9]

Kantian aesthetics conducts an exploration of the structure of representation itself and not just its content. Thus the aesthetic may be considered as a branch of knowledge that exists alongside the epistemological and the ethical. Contemporaries of Kant, like Friedrich Schelling and S. T. Coleridge, in fact,

---

[5] Terry Eagleton, *The Ideology of the Aesthetic,* 87.

[6] "For the imagination, in accordance with the laws of association, makes our state of contentment dependent on physical conditions. But acting in accordance with the principles of the schematism of judgement […] it is at the same time an instrument of reason and its ideas." Immanuel Kant, *The Critique of Judgement,* 121.

[7] Theodor Adorno, *Philosophy of Modern Music,* 18.

[8] John Cage, *Silence,* 171. See also in this publication David Hanner's and John Wall's "The Material Experience of Abstraction", 92.

[9] Immanuel Kant, *The Critique of Judgement,* 71 (my emphasis).

believed the aesthetic to underpin all other forms of knowledge, but of course neither of these thinkers was able to figure the aesthetic in terms other than some kind of transcendental, even semi-divine subject. It took Arthur Schopenhauer to disengage the reflexivity of the aesthetic from subjectivity. Schopenhauer argued in a way that is similar to poststructuralism that it is through representation that there is a reality. Representation itself is structured according to the subject / object dichotomy and categorical rules like the principle of sufficient reason.[10] However, Schopenhauer argues that to insist there is no reality which is not at the same time an object of representation is to invite serious psychiatric disturbance.[11] To accept this would mean that the body exists purely in terms of the objectifying categories of rationalist and idealist philosophy. Of course we do know our bodies as objects, and the social construction of the body occurs through the internalization of representations. On the other hand, however, the body constitutes a condition or representation, necessary but not sufficient, just as language upon deconstructive analysis reveals the body as a kind of trace. For Schopenhauer then the knowledge of the body is always also an immediate form of knowledge, unknowable except in representation but nonetheless not exhausted by the same representation.[12]

Music in Schopenhauer is nonrepresentational, immediate knowledge, meaning that it may be construed as an exploration, amongst other things, of sensuous or aesthetic knowledge, the conditions of representation. Schopenhauer follows the Kantian system in so far as he aims towards an explication of the conditions of knowledge, but he turns the vertigo-prone Kant on his head. Where Kant supposes these *a priori* conditions to be categories of knowledge derived from the tradition of Aristotelean logic, Schopenhauer looks to music, arguing that it is the *a priori* form of a sensuous, bodily knowledge that conditions all cognitive activity.[13]

One of the criticisms levelled at Schopenhauer's theory of music is that it construes music as a metaphysical entity, whose meaning or function is always said to exist in some kind of shadowy, noumenal world beyond the empirical. According to Vladimir Jankélévitch, this is to miss the metaphorical dimension of music:

> A sonata *is like* a précis of the human adventure at is bordered by birth and death—but is not *itself* this adventure. The *Allegro maestoso* and the Adagio—

---

[10] Arthur Schopenhauer, *The World as Will and Representation* Vol. I, 5-6.
[11] "As a serious conviction ... [solipsism] could be found only in a madhouse; as such it would then need not so much a refutation as a cure." Arthur Schopenhauer, *Ibid,* 104.
[12] Arthur Schopenhauer, *Ibid,* 19-20.
[13] Arthur Schopenhauer, *Ibid,* 256-257.

Schopenhauer wants to write their metaphysics—are like a stylization of the two tempos of experienced time, but they are not themselves this time itself.[14]

Thus Schopenhauer is accused of forgetting that for all its philosophical a *priori* character of immediacy, music always occurs in a representational medium. It is a valid criticism, but to be fair to Schopenhauer he never supposed that "immediacy" could be manifested in any other way than as a representation, just as for Nietzsche, the Apollonian is the expression of the Dionysian. At a philosophical level, music, for Schopenhauer, is always a reflexive representation; the most reflexive in fact given that as an expressive form it is not tied to signifying categories like metaphor and analogy in the same way language is. However, in addition, much rests on what is understood by the term "metaphor". If it is simply the transposition of a number of likenesses from one system of expression to another, then Jankélélevitch may be said to have misread Schopenhauer. If on the other hand, metaphor is understood as a dynamic component in the generation of meaning as Jacques Lacan,[15] following Roman Jacobsen, proposes then we simply need to remind ourselves, that Schopenhauer's immediacy is not of Platonic transcendence but of the body, sensuality, the Will; perhaps more eco-warrior than connoisseur of rarified nothingness: "I recognize in the deepest tones of harmony, in the ground-bass, the lowest grades of the will's objectification, inorganic nature, the mass of the planet."[16]

French philosopher Maurice Merleau-Ponty may be said to take up the Schopenhauerian thesis on music, body and knowledge in his argument that the poignancy and radical impact of music is directed towards the body, and on it, opens up an original event of ideation. In order to explicate the relation between the world of signification and the body, Merleau-Ponty draws on the expressive differences between the impact a piece of music may have on a person and its subsequent explication in objective form. Marcel Proust's character, Swann, is captivated by a piece of music. It is real to him, substantial and positive, yet it is different from the experience of reflective knowledge about music. Merleau-Ponty argues that the "little" phrase, as Swann calls it, is simultaneously "ideal" and "carnal". If it were not of the body, it would not move us, and detached from carnality it would lose its affectivity. But neither is it purely of the body; it is of a world of meaning, in the same way as is

---

[14] Vladimir Jankélévitch, *Music and the Ineffable,* 14.

[15] Jacques Lacan, *Ecrits,* 298.

[16] Arthur Schopenhauer, *The World as Will and Representation,* 258.

the first vision, the first pleasure", an initiation, "an opening of a dimension that can never be closed, the establishment of a level in terms of which every other experience will henceforth be situated.[17]

This level or dimension of experience is that of non-cognitive ideation, or perception without cognition, which is conditioned by the perceptual world but not reducible to it. On the contrary, while it is expressive of the being of the body, it also renders the body and the world of things intelligible. Here we encounter the possibility of embarking on a dialectic of body and spirit, which in my opinion, would be the best way to destroy both Merleau-Ponty's and Schopenhauer's insights. Merleau-Ponty, recognising the allure of the regressive dialectic and philosophy's inability to conceive adequately the processes of mediation, introduces a subtle logical figure, the chiasm. It is a figure that at once accommodates the logic of continuity in mediation, while at the same time expressing difference. Hence, to use Merleau-Ponty's example, when I touch something; that something is also touching me; I am touched by the smooth, cool warmth of the tea-cup that I drink from, as if the cup had skin. The experience of identity and difference in touching-being-touched, seeing-being-seen renders perception not primarily as either active or passive, as in Berkley, but as an opening or fold in the field of experience, a "dehiscence". This intertwining of the elements that constitute perception and thought is in Merleau-Ponty's vocabulary, flesh; a flesh whose structure is chiasmatic, not wholly material, not wholly intelligibility:

> There is a strict ideality in experiences that are experiences of the flesh: the moments of the sonata, the fragments of the luminous field, adhere to one another with a cohesion without concept, which is of the same type as the cohesion of the parts of my body with the world. Is my body a thing, is it an idea? It is neither, being the measurant of the things. We will therefore have to recognize an ideality that is not alien to the flesh that gives it its axes, its depth, its dimension.[18]

The chiasmic figure, considered as an elemental threshold point intertwining intelligible and sensuous form, is an attempt to think the non-signifying component of signification, that element of meaning which, in fact, does not register on the logic-governed screen of the received practices of signification. An approach such as this must deal with the binary oppositions and dualisms upon which signifying systems are constructed—mind / body, man / woman, good / evil, signifier / signified. The chiasm attempts to neutralise the mutually exclusive logic (the so-called excluded middle) and hierarchy implicit in these

---

[17] Maurice Merleau-Ponty, *The Visible and the Invisible,* 151.
[18] Maurice Merleau-Ponty, *Ibid,* 152.

distinctions as well as provide a set of pathways for thinking intelligently about non-signifying symbolic systems, or at least, their non-signifying dimension.

There is implicit in music, Jankélévitch reminds us, a propensity to collapse the binary system of logic that governs linguistic, cultural and psychological signification:

> The musical universe, not signifying any particular meaning, is first of all the antipode to any coherent system... Harmony itself is less the rational synthesis of opposites than the irrational symbiosis of the heterogeneous... Music, like movement or duration, is a continuous miracle that with every step accomplishes the impossible. The superimposed voices of polyphony realize a *concordia discors,* of which music alone is capable, because intelligent articulation based on reciprocity, because the meshed gears of question and answer in dialogue, differ as much from the synchronism of heterogeneous voices in counterpoint as the "harmony" one produces by adjudication differs from musical harmony.[19]

Thus aesthetic discourse on music may be directed to a structural analysis of the musical representation and its relation to other signifying systems. Here, in direct contrast to language, music tends not to bring about its harmonic and discordant synthesis through the reduction of elements to mutually exclusive, irreducible opposites. In fact, according to Jankélévitch, it is not really correct to speak of synthesis in relation to music. It is the contention of this paper that the "miracle" spoken of in the quote above may be construed in terms of a general debate on signification. It is what Schopenhauer meant when he spoke of music as an *a priori* language of the body that is both representational and nonrepresentational, a geometry which contains within itself its own fluidity of line and plane. It is a geometry of illusion, of parallel universes. Merleau-Ponty's chiasm aims at the same ontological space as do a host of other such concepts elaborated in early twentieth-century psychology and late twentieth century philosophy and literary theory.[20] Another more contemporary formulation of the same problem may be found in Gilles Deleuze's and Félix Guattari's concept of "Body without Organs."

The chiasm of course demonstrates the logical circularity of the general figure of the logical paradox, where a thing may be simultaneously big and small, flesh and spirit, inside and outside, discordant and harmonious. Unfortunately, however, the term has a very low level of psychological and logical resonance. It smoothes the world into a multiplicity of convergence and divergence. It conjures, and this is perhaps unfair to Merleau-Ponty, the calm exchanges of positive and negative electrons. This is the disadvantage of

---

[19] Vladimir Jankélévitch, *Music and the Ineffable,* 18-19.
[20] For a productive treatment of this history see chapters 1-3 of Merleau-Ponty's *Phenomenology of Perception,* Trans. Colin Smith (London: Routledge, 1962).

designating ontologically significant events with terms that have little to do with everyday experience. It lacks intensity. Schopenhauer, in addition to speaking of a musical *a priori* and the force of the Will, also spoke of the psychiatric consequences of internalising the view that all is representation, that there is no non-signifying element which can not be objectified through the lucid calculus of sufficient reason.[21] It is the fault-line of this disturbance as much as the *a priori* character of music that must be attended to in aesthetic discourse. For, indeed, the structure of contemporary knowledge and society does in fact demand the devolution of knowledge onto cognitive capacity and the rendering of the body according to categories of epistemology and social-ethical norms. The glass bodies and sprung bodies of Descartes's madmen are not just dramatic counter examples to the sanity of the *cogito*, but logical consequences of the intense rigor of the Cartesian system as it seeks to invent the subject of knowledge in the image of mathematical abstraction. It is in fact Deleuze and Guattari's "Body without Organs" that conveys the paradoxical qualities, logical and existential, necessary for an aesthetic discourse that both collapses the binary oppositions of signification and delivers the necessary psychological, semantic and social "jolt" implicit in such collapse:

> A BwO is made in such a way that it can be occupied, populated only by intensities... The BwO is not a scene, a place, or even a support upon which something comes to pass. It has nothing to do with phantasy, there is nothing to interpret ... it is not space; it is matter that occupies space to a given degree... That is why we treat the BwO as the full egg before the extension of the organism and the organization of the organs, before the formation of the strata; as the intense egg defined by axes and vectors, gradients and thresholds, by dynamic tendencies involving energy transformation and kinematic movements involving group displacements, by migrations: all independent of *accessory forms* because the organs appear and function here as pure intensities.[22]

The concept BwO has been received as something of a moveable feast. Make of it what you will! It thus contains the potential for its own meaninglessness. However, there are several key points that render it of significance in aesthetic discourse. It is an example of "concrete ontology"; that is, it constitutes an exploration of the conditions of signification, recognizing that meaning is made up of bits and pieces of material that are invested with symbolic vitality, like the universe. A word is a thing. A musical note is a sound long before it is ever a cognition, as Morton Feldman insisted upon. It is an element in the Empedoclean sense, meaningful, but not in the sense that it signifies anything in particular. The BwO is a playful convergence onto some kind of nexus that in

---

[21] Arthur Schopenhauer, *The World as Will and Representation,* 104.
[22] Gilles Deleuze and Félix Guattari, *A Thousand Plateaus,* 153.

turn generates meaning by whatever means available to it. It is a metaphor, yes. What else could an egg be doing in theoretical discourse? Lewis Carroll was familiar with this kind of argument. But in addition, it expresses simply the power of metaphor to generate meaning, signification. Moreover, as a description, it sounds like music, like Vladimir Jankélévitch's description of music as the collapse of signification. And crucially, as an aesthetic concept, it detaches judgement from the self-righteous moral subject and projects it back onto the collective, to the "mass of the planet" as Schopenhauer put it. And, as much as Schopenhauer has been lambasted for his aesthetic approach, it is not possible to conceive of music as metamorphosis, using the terms of a discourse that would preclude the possibility of hearing in music the "the mass of the planet", or indeed, as in Deleuze and Guattari's case, the intensity of a criss-crossed egg. Kant launched his aesthetic philosophy in the right direction, towards an analysis of what is after all the formal qualities of metamorphosis—the transformative, world-making capacity of representation. But he pulled up short, circumscribing his immensely powerful and creative aesthetic discourse with the propriety of the Enlightenment citizen. How else would the punctilious Kant deal with Echoes, Narcissuses, nymphs, forest spirits and shape-changing water?

II

These introductory remarks are in no way intended to serve as a framework for the interpretation of the essays gathered in this publication. It serves rather as a point of departure. At the philosophical level, these essays test and utilise the assumption that music is less a representational than an existential and highly particular perspective on the social-symbolic system. Thus, music does not so much reflect society, or a state of affairs, as make a significant contribution to the way in which things come to acquire meaning—aesthetic, personal, political, ideological, economic and scientific.

While these essays follow a particular cluster of themes, the musical focus is diverse, and covers rap, rock, pop, metal, new music, classical music and music video. The specific discourses are oriented towards the politics of composition and performance on the one hand, and the interpretation, dissemination and institutionalization of musical practices, on the other hand. All of these essays in their own pay pick up on the contradictions, paradoxes and impasses that characterize the musical form. The most obvious examples of this "unease" derive from the fact that this highly aesthetic and deeply personal art form normally functions in the context of a multibillion dollar industry, powerful social institutions like universities and an environment of political and social conflict, prejudice and discrimination. On top of everything else, music is "uplifting", it gives hope, expresses longing and desire. Perhaps the chief focus of these papers, collectively and individually, is that music is eclectic, often despite itself, and pulls into its orbit whatever is loosed upon the social sphere, from physics, epidemics, racism, psychological breakdown, belief, money and ideology.

The central paradox of the first essay by Dafydd Jones is that of how minority linguistic, ethnic and social groups opposed to the standardisation of experience may simultaneously invigorate a dominant culture in a dominant language without at the same time diminishing the invigorating voice of the minority voice. The imperialism of dominant languages like English, for example, lives off both the rich contributions of minority languages and cultural practices that come its way, and ultimately, as history has shown, destroys them. There is such a thing as an imperialist metabolism. Jones argues that in the context of Welsh music and the fraught issue of language, the minority voice may simply operate as a tolerated guest, able in fact, because of this status, to bring about no real change. On the other hand, the stated aim of bringing about change in a revolutionary way, in the face of the behemoth, may be a self-satisfying illusion. Rather, using the concept of minorisation borrowed from Gilles Deleuze and Félix Guattari, the minority voice, in Welsh or English, sustains itself and brings about real change to the degree that it relieves the imperialistic medium of the belief that it is a central organizing principle around which minorities cluster, even if to protest. Minority music, therefore, is not simply the voice of an ethnic identity threatened with debilitating change. Minorities change too, not necessarily according to the dictates of enormous concentrations of power, but according to their own sense of who they are and will be.

John MacKay, a former student of Californian composer, Robert Erickson, traces the institutional pressures on composers of new music during the 1960s and 1970s to concentrate themselves in ever-expanding blocks of influence and style, which would vindicate imperialist drift. The counter culture that is often spoken of in relation to the California of this period in history is subject to the law that sociologists call institutionalization. So, for example, once an ecology party enters parliament, it will lose its ability for radical grassroots action, because one half is making the policies that the other half opposes. It is also the case with music. In order to avoid this kind of situation in music, Erickson stayed aloof from "schools" of music, favouring the smaller and more spontaneous "scene", despite its often fleeting nature and institutional insecurity. MacKay tells the story of Erickson in a biographical mode, the beauty being that it becomes possible to note and plot the myriad of influences that perpetually transformed the life of a single individual, where this myriad of influences is preserved in the dynamic "sound snapshot", which is Erickson's music.

One of the most knotty issues in music criticism, especially as it is practiced in cultural studies, is the reconciliation of artistic creativity and social-political efficaciousness with large amounts of money. It is strange that this question rarely comes up in relation to other arts, even other kinds of music. While Herbert von Karajan became extremely wealthy through music, the quality of his ability to interpret and conduct music is never really brought into question, although there is dissatisfaction with his cynicism. And it is not imagined that because he was rolling in money, Picasso was a lesser painter. In rock music, however, it takes very little in the way of success to generate cries of "sellout". Rodney Sharkey investigates this phenomenon, quickly seeing off the theoretical arguments both against the influence of capital and in favour of the strategic consumption of popular music. The author makes two telling points. David Bowie, the subject of the essay, is no innocent actor plying his critical trade only to be absorbed by the system in his later years. Bowie is part of the system. He reflects it from within, draws on its resources, transforms and exploits it. He is at once a social agent and a theatrical figure responding to the processes and forces of symbolic change. In this sense, Bowie embodies the cultural and semantic practice of metamorphosis. Sharkey's second point is that the precariousness of the study of popular music forces the critic to acknowledge the social, intellectual and symbolic conditions under which theory is developed for the interpretation of culture. Thus popular music criticism is a testing ground not only for the music, but for theory itself, as Adorno insisted must be the case in all music criticism, despite his own blindspots.

The rhetorical and performative affect of Heavy Metal is subjected to scrutiny in an essay which poses questions arising out of the convergence of the self-proclaimed revolutionary aims, fascist rhetoric, and capitalistic means of Nordic Metal. İbrahim Beyazoğlu offers an in-depth analysis of the cycle of Norwegian Metal from its novel radicalism in the early 1980s, the church-burning, fascist "other-hating" middle period to the quiet of what turned out to be prison for some, wealth for others. He offers an interpretation of the Nordic Metal absorption of Norse mythology and the proclamations that would see a return to what were perceived to be pagan values, values which are gleaned and developed upon slim evidence and highly selective readings of the myths, mediated as they are by infantile 1940s fascists like Vidmund Quisling and, ironically, their Christian originators. Beyazoğlu examines both the self-mythologization of the Metal movement in Norway and its complicity in the system it purported to loath. Also brought into question here is the capacity of critical discourse on popular music to do anything other than build a political alliance with one side or the other of the argument such that critical discourse would become an extension of the culture industry, with little real independence of mind. For Beyazoğlu, critical independence is not equivalent to a spurious impartiality. It comes from the imaginative internalisation of ambiguity and radical uncertainty.

Contemporary cultural studies is attuned to the environment of conflict in which much music is produced. There is no need to rehearse arguments about the role of music in countering the mind-numbing propaganda of various dictatorial regimes as well as the suffocating emptiness and misinformation of not so dictatorial regimes in their bid to manipulate public opinion. Moreover, the cathartic quality of music is more and more being drawn into professional psychotherapy, not simply to sooth but to bring about transformations in deeply traumatized subjects where more orthodox, cognitive methods fail. Vincent Meelberg explores accounts of the psychology of trauma, not so much in order to advance therapeutic practice, as to interrogate the representational structure of music, asking what would be required for music itself to internalise characteristics of trauma. It is a venture that is theoretically possible. Interestingly, however, once Meelberg has established a "grammar" of trauma at the level of musicology, he finds that it is not possible to contrive a music that would conform to these requirements, without, that is, getting in with Pythagoras and proposing a music that was an embodiment of time itself, a music without difference, like an eternity spent in solitary confinement with *Einstein on the Beach*. Alternatively, Meelberg concludes that trauma may be expressed or embodied in music through musical anomaly—stray sounds, gaps and interruption to the general structure of the musical phrase.

The subject of rock music video comes up in Rodney Sharkey's discussion of David Bowie. Sharkey sees Bowie's innovation in music video in the shift from visual narrative to visual symbol and metaphor, a movement not necessarily related to a narrative telos that would unfold in a formal sequence. To borrow from poetry, Bowie inaugurates the lyric video. Video auteur Chris Cunningham operates in a similar visual environment. According to Tristan Fidler, Cunningham generates a hermetic spatial world in which his subjects inhere as if purely through the forces of the environment, devoid of active, projective subjectivity. This "laboratory," however, is forged from the familiar urban environment. As they move through this world, which, temporally, is like a stream that flows within a confined space and therefore flows nowhere, *always*, the body of the subject takes on the elemental characteristics of the surrounding world. One set of bodies takes on fluid qualities, while another fractures under its own brittleness. The argument here is that Cunningham, by infusing the digital body with the varied rhythms of music, conjures a drama of the imaginary body. The space, subjectivity and body of Cunningham's film is not necessarily an imaginative counterpart to concrete experience. The imaginary here, as in the case of Lacanian psychoanalytic theory, is implicit in the real, not as a possibility but as a permanent feature of its construction. Thus the music video constitutes a musical form that articulates the embrace of the virtual and the actual, dissolving for the duration of the video the binary oppositions that structure the practices of signification. In this way Cunningham's video is the creation of a dream form particular to the visual medium and according to the fluid, non-signifying logic of music.

Jankélévitch says of music that it brings about the dissolution of the subject. In Cunningham's videos the loss of self is irredeemable and traumatic, and the body is reduced to an element that is organized externally. There are instances when it is the desired outcome of music, when the ego is replaced by the materiality of music: "the man robbed of a self ... has become nothing more than a vibrating string, a sounding pipe."[23] For American composer, Morton Feldman, the aim of composition was the return of the material to music so that composer, listener or performer could enter into its sonic being unencumbered by symbols and historical complexes. Feldman recognises that the relation of sonic material and the signifying functions of music are deeply interlocked and so he placed at the centre of his compositional method a paradox; namely that the route to the material is through the abstract. Feldman does not here refer to mathematical abstraction. Rather, in order to return sound to music as he sees it, Feldman studies its form, its duration, its production in space and as a thing, its silence. David Hanner and John Wall argue silence is a kind of dehiscence, an opening of meaning onto the material, in this case the body.

In the second of the essays to deal specifically with aesthetics, and the last essay in the collection, Paal Fagerheim adopts an approach that would seem to be diametrically opposed to that of silence. In fact, the aesthetics of noise and silence are intimately related especially in the work of John Cage, for whom silence was the eradication of crusty musical convention, the removal of which allowed music to be heard as noise. Fagerheim's analysis of noise insists on the social dimension. Here music is eclectic and mimetic of the discordance and volume of society. Public Enemy engages directly with the hostile world of American social politics. In order to do justice to this, Fagerheim devises a method that brings to bear formal musical analysis onto the noise-producing frictions of society, and thus is produced, at a theoretical level, a musical analysis of society, as if it were music, which it is. Thus Public Enemy produces simultaneously the most radical and the most traditional of music, a music whose *a priori* of enunciation inheres in society, its clamour and its silence.

John Wall
Eastern Mediterranean University

---

[23] Vladimir Jankélévitch, *Music and the Ineffable,* 1.

References

Adorno, Theodor. *Philosophy of Modern Music.* Trans. Anne Mitchell and Wesley Blomster. New York: Continuum, 1973.

Deleuze, Gilles and Félix Guattari. *A Thousand Plateaus: Capitalism and Schizophrenia.* Trans. Brian Masumi. Minneapolis: University of Minneapolis Press, 1994.

Cage, John. *Silence.* Middletown, Connecticut: Wesleyan University Press, 1961.

Eagleton, Terry. *The Ideology of the Aesthetic.* Oxford: Basil Blackwell, 1990.

Frith, Simon. "Defending Popular Culture from the Populists." *Diacritics* 21 (1991): 102-115.

Jankélévitch, Vladimir. *Music and the Ineffable.* Trans. Carolyn Abbate. Princeton: Princeton University Press, 2003.

Kant, Immanuel. *The Critique of Judgement.* Trans. James Creed. Oxford: Clarendon Press, 1991.

Lacan, Jacques. *Écrits: A Selection.* Trans. Alan Sheridan. London: W. W. Norton & Company, 1977.

Merleau-Ponty, Maurice. *The Visible and the Invisible.* Trans. Alphonso Lingis. Evanston: Northwestern University Press, 1968.

Schopenhauer, Arthur. *The World as Will and Representation,* Volume I. Trans. E. F. J. Payne. New York: Dover Publications, 1966.

CHAPTER ONE

THE INTERNATIONAL LANGUAGE OF SCREAMING: HOLEY SPACE AND MINORISATION IN MUSIC AND LANGUAGE

DAFYDD JONES

Abstract: Certain actions and positions are perceived in the world of music as radical and even revolutionary. Of course a single action may be radical at any one time and place, reactionary at other times and places, or otherwise totally meaningless. This essay interrogates the validity of claims made in the name of radical intervention in musical practice, linking the analysis of the politics of music to language and its minorisation, itself always a process, a becoming and never an identity. Minorisation, borrowed from Deleuze and Guattari, rejects the subject position of spokesperson, and instead critically engages with a dominant or standardised cultural, musical or linguistic form, deterritorialising the field, opening up pathways, eroding others and ultimately determining the hegemonic form as virtual, no longer actual. Welsh band, the Super Furry Animals don't smash their guitars; they operate in a precarious, dynamic space where identities and languages are forged and come asunder, between languages, cultures and musical constituencies. There is no classical revolution here, no supplanting of the old order with the self-evidently moral and cosmic superiority of the new. The old binaries are dissolved into ephemera, but remain real nonetheless, and the "minorist" reinvigorates the dominant form, while at the same time thwarting its resurgent imperialism. Dafydd Jones directs revolutionary cultural activity towards the generation of new meaning; semiosis, as opposed to the overthrowing or even subverting of received practices.

In the early twentieth century, dada *manifesteur* Tristan Tzara goaded musicians to smash their blind instruments on stage in aggravated provocation of, ultimately, state power.[1] It is unlikely that Tzara's haranguing of the audience at the Cabaret Voltaire anticipated the instrumental carnage that became a tiresomely familiar event on music stages later in the same century, destruction predictable to the point that it no longer posed any kind of cultural or political

---

[1] Tristan Tzara, *Seven Dada Manifestos*, 16.

significance or threat, and impotent as an extravagant oppositional pose. Trying to figure out what meant anything in the music that I not only heard but crucially *saw* growing up in the 1970s and 1980s wasn't easy (and was compounded by being geographically located out on a "provincial" limb). In one brief but memorable phase at Cardiff's main music venue, it appeared to mean nothing when a series of white Stratocasters were smashed in encore at a Ritchie Blackmore's Rainbow concert; there was, surely, more to it when The Vibrators' John Ellis axed his guitar in my face in 1980; Peter Gabriel cracking my head with his searchlight during an unconventional stage entry left me slightly off kilter; and when Motorhead came to town, the concert hall roof actually caved in—things at that point looked promising.[2] In a particular sense, those early and eclectic live music forays were concerned with the *effect* of the event, which continually deflected any concern with what the event *meant*, and in their direct and active modes they expressed some nascent physical interventionist mode against, yes, state power, doing so in a form that itself prefigured an alternative.

After the concert hall's collapse and eventual demolition in the wake of Motorhead, there was no obvious successor as a music venue for Anglo-American hegemony in Cardiff (though such venues were safely reinstituted within a decade or so). The possibility of alterity seemed at the time a necessary position to maintain, and charting the *terra incognita* of disused docklands led perhaps inevitably to a one-time nonconformist chapel building now barely altered for the purposes of live music performance (which, incidentally, was *not* congregational singing) and other "attendant" activities—the seductively named and dimly lit *Casablanca* club, where I remember on one occasion facing ejection in no uncertain terms for wearing threatening shoes. The music I heard and saw there came from very different places to the other stuff encountered up until that point, an alternative and unlicenced hybrid ground that posed something radical in its difference. A discussion as to *why* such alterity seemed then, and still seems, a given and necessary part of music will be reserved in this essay, in order to establish rather a primary focus on the question of *how* such alterity might be possible within the familiar stalemate of oppositionality (occupied by most—increasingly all?—western music today). What follow here are considerations that do not arise uniquely in the context of music, but are in certain terms exemplified through the musical instances isolated, emergent as they are from the seedbed and system of western popular music and all that comes with it. To this extent, the appeal at the outset is to cede the impossibility of a system that has no outside (the outside being a fundamental requisite of

---

[2] This is not a joke. But to clarify, on 10 January 1982, the roof of the Sophia Gardens Pavilion collapsed under the weight of snow.

oppositionality), because even when the margin or periphery might disappear, there will always be holes out of which all manner of subjects might emerge.

Holey bombs make holey holes

The punctured space named "holey" by Gilles Deleuze and Félix Guattari is space that permits movement, but distinctly within demarcations:[3] what it allows us initially to conceptualise is a spatial resistance to totality, a resistance however potentially stifled by structuralist "tolerance" of radical difference. Tolerance here is such that it will always and without compromise reimpose the regulating authority of the structure if ever any actual threat beyond the gestural is sensed, and the freedom to move is, accordingly, virtual. Cultural demarcations are at best contingent—at least one among our most influential thinkers on "culture" wound up wishing he had never even heard the damned word[4]—and any return on our cultural investment poses particular problems: the stakes in the production of culture, for example, are rarely, if ever, visible. The assumption that we all, broadly speaking, share the same political stakes deliberately gets in the way of specifying or concretising what the stakes might be in any given cultural situation, and problematically underlies the generation through social mechanisms of what is the both dismissive and exonerating "power of oblivion":[5] the immediate response under the conditions that arise from such an assumption invariably comes in one form or another of the declaration that *this problem does not concern me*. As an indicator, indeed, of the politically marginal status of minority culturally specific production (even though your minority may be my dominant), it is framed for discussion precisely as a problem that does not concern its nominal "public", for whom it proceeds to circulate as politically impotent and also as culturally phatic, its difference tolerated by the cursory nod.

The difficulty is that the assumption assumes that my stakes are the same as yours, and what allows the assumption to be made is a tolerance that is always

---

[3] Deleuze and Guattari, *A Thousand Plateaus*, 351–423.

[4] Raymond Williams, *Politics and Letters*, 154: "Culture: I don't know how many times I wish I'd never heard the damned word."

[5] The idea of the power of oblivion is developed in the work of French theorist Guy Hocquenghem, and his theoretical trilogy *Le désir homosexuel* (1972*), L'Après-Mai des faunes* (1974), *and Le dérive homosexuelle* (1977), which together comprise a radical critique of Freudian psychoanalytic theory and liberal social theory from a Marxist perspective, providing analysis therein of the role of the state and civil society in the determination of "identity politics". Only the first of these three tracts has been translated into English, as *Homosexual Desire* (trans. Danielle Dangoor, London: Allison and Busby, 1978).

and purely nominal—a virtual tolerance "because real tolerance would be a contradiction in terms". To tolerate, then, would not be to extend the gesture of support, but rather to *condemn*. Pier Paolo Pasolini elucidates the point, observing how

> they tell the "tolerated" person to do as he wishes, that he has every right to follow his own nature, that the fact that he belongs to a minority does not in the least mean inferiority, etc. But his "difference"—or better, his "crime of being different"—remains the same both with regard to those who have decided to tolerate him and those who have decided to condemn him. No majority will ever be able to banish from its consciousness the feeling of the "difference" of minorities.[6]

Figure 1: Still from Sergei Eisenstein's *Strike*

Tolerance then masks the imposition of identity by others upon the individual (as different or as belonging to a minority), and though the consequences may at turns be dire, it is questionable whether the individual ever finds him- or herself in a position practically to exercise the undeniable right to *refuse* any imposed identity. The problematic nature of a contemporary individual identity in a hybrid society, however, compounds concerns over imposition and refusal by the question of *who* or *which constituency* is addressed by the "tolerated" person; if a "tolerated" musician, for instance, sings to a specific constituency, we ought to ask how he or she has taken account of where that constituency is to be found, or how that constituency is to be constructed—because the cultural producer is always in a position of constructing the constituency.

The minority status of the "tolerated" person is now perhaps a poorly defined proposition, constructed just as the constituency is constructed, and one that has confused rather than clarified anything for itself in recent years by groping around critical theoretical ideas in the hope that the result will pass for a

---

[6] Pier Paolo Pasolini, "Grenneriello", 21–22.

conceptually consistent and coherent account. Beneath the overarching and sometimes (if not always) *too* convenient "postmodern sensibility" (whatever that term might assume to refer to—in practical instantiation, it appears to function as a vague, to the point of being useless, theoretical catch-all), we are given readings that almost indiscriminately cover every base from *authenticity* to *otherness* to *postcolonialism*, and that collectively amount to what might most succinctly be described as decidedly *un*critical theory, as they submit to an out-of-focus ideology. But beginning to correct such unchecked drift, and to move towards reestablishing a theoretically sound reading of what "minority" refers to, first demands that we make consistent our invocation of the notion of "majority" as the counter to "minority" and as the pretext for democracy— "majority" then as a standard or model, rather than as a quantity of people. The model, definitionally, does not demand greater numbers to secure its majority[7] status—the masses, we are reminded, are restrained from forming the majority—but is constituted as the opposite to a multiplicity of social or cultural "minority" formations; each formation is a formation in process, in Deleuzean terms, a *becoming-minor*, the example demonstrating that "there is a becoming-woman of men (but no becoming-man of women, masculinity being a constituent part of the standard)".[8]

What this proposes is a sense of "minority" that makes little use of fixity in defining itself; rather, its continual process indicates "a combination of active forces, of forces for change", and the creativity in minority lies precisely in this collective force for change. As such, it drives *against* the stability of claims for continuity that are conventionally related by minority representations posing as some kind of self-styled cultural custodians, and in so doing it questions the validity of those "minority" claims. The effect, as Jean-Jacques Lecercle has clarified, is to put the minority identity into crisis when its distinct status relative to the majority is lost:

> nobody is a member of the majority (hence its famed "silence"), as everybody is caught in some sort of becoming-minor. And, contrary to appearances, the left's appeal to "the people" is not an appeal to the majority ... but an appeal to the potential for change of an array of creative minorities.[9]

Recognising the creativity of minority in terms of what I have just described poses a direct threat to the cultural relevance of continued minority cultural production, as it exposes the unsound base upon which a "united minorities front" is assembled, and from which disparate minority voices are said to be

---

[7] SFA, "The Man Don't give a Fuck": "Out of focus ideology / Keep the masses from majority."

[8] Jean-Jacques Lecercle, *Deleuze and Language*, 194.

[9] Jean-Jacques Lecercle, *Ibid*, 194.

raised—unsound because the majority against which the minority can only cohere becomes unrecognisable when we are all of us bound up in becoming-minor.

Holey holes make homeless moles

Deleuze and Guattari advance the concept of "minor literature"—that is to say the work called minor, as opposed to notions of "minor literary classics" or any attempt "to put *Metamorphoses* in the same category as *Lorna Doone*"[10]—in their 1975 work on Kafka, exposing "literature" as a social product to the contingencies and differences of its constituent parts. In working through the concept with reference to language and written, literary matter, it is apposite here to approach minorisation in music beginning with the *vox humana* and the words that are performed. Deleuze and Guattari exercise a revision of the entire economy of language and literature generally as a centre of subjectification, to reinstitute the subject particularly as the *centre* of language:

> How many people today live in a language that is not their own? Or no longer, or not yet, even know their own and know poorly the major language that they are forced to use? This is the problem ... of minorities, the problem of a minor literature, but also a problem for all of us: how to tear a minor literature away from its own language, allowing it to challenge the language and making it follow a sober revolutionary path.[11]

The minority deployment of a non-minority language, Deleuze and Guattari suggest, is not the result of the subject's aesthetic choice and exercising of will, but rather it is the result of an exigency. The existential situation in which the "minor" subject finds him- or herself is crucially not one of possessing an abstract universal (a single national language or cultural identity), with the result being that a new economy of production and reception is called into being.

"Minor literature", as described in *Kafka: Toward a Minor Literature*, is not literature written in the minor (or minority) language, but "is rather that which a minority constructs in a major language".[12] As the above extract indicates, observation of the minorisation that occurs within a language needs somehow to negotiate means beyond supplication to that language, so that the minor variant

---

[10] Jean-Jacques Lecercle, *Ibid*, 194. Something is lost in translation into English from the original French, and such reference to "minor literature" can, of course, be misleading. For Deleuze and Guattari, an artist is great because minor; the focus in their collaborative work falls on Kafka, then effecting "an inversion of the usual phrase, "a minor classic," which they blissfully ignore, as it has no equivalent in French". *Ibid*, 194.

[11] Deleuze and Guattari, *Kafka*, 19.

[12] Deleuze and Guattari, *Ibid*, 16.

can begin to effect change in the realms of production and consumption. The instance that would situate the present discussion on recognisable terrain (for the author at least) is of the Welsh band, Super Furry Animals, in whose music "the equally weighted importance of local culture and internationally shared popular culture" is implicit.[13] Critical to the music is its linguistic medium—English—which is not the language that the members of the band speak to one another in: speaking in Welsh, singing in English, SFA do something with their music surmounting a series of "impossibilities" that, similarly, once posed themselves before Kafka. Franz Kafka was a Czech and a Jew who spoke Czech and Yiddish, but he set aside those languages to write in a foreign language; the sequence of "impossibilities" he encountered, suggest Deleuze and Guattari, were the "impossibility of not writing ... the impossibility of writing other than in German ... the impossibility of writing in German".[14] By its fluid state, intermixing with the others, the situation of the German language in Prague under the Hapsburg Monarchy, with "a withered vocabulary, an incorrect syntax",[15] productively though paradoxically allowed Kafka the possibility of invention.[16] Now, for German read English as the "paper language" of present concern, and the proposition that the "impossibility" of not writing (songs) recurs for Super Furry Animals whose textual matter today reaffirms, intentionally or otherwise, how "national consciousness, uncertain or oppressed, necessarily exists by means of literature"[17] in a country that remains colonial and colonised.

The SFA example gains little through any appeal to the making audible of minority voices in a conventional sense—indeed, the previous section demonstrates the redundancy of the idea of "minority", which has long since been overtaken by the condition becoming-minor. The currency of two languages simultaneously poses a provocative duality, as SFA, in repose, first employ a language that actually has a history of being oppressed and persecuted

---

[13] Griffiths and Hill, "Postcolonial Music", 229.

[14] Deleuze and Guattari, *Kafka*, 16.

[15] Deleuze and Guattari, *Ibid*, 22. The analysis of Prague German by Klaus Wagenbach throws up "the incorrect use of prepositions; the abuse of the pronominal; the employment of malleable verbs [...]; the multiplication and succession of adverbs; the use of pain-filled connotations; the importance of the accent as a tension internal to the word; and the distribution of consonants and vowels as part of an internal discordance. Wagenbach insists on this point: all these marks of the poverty of a language show up in Kafka but have been taken over by a creative utilisation for the purposes of a new sobriety, a new expressivity, a new flexibility, a new intensity." Deleuze and Guattari, *Ibid*, 23, referencing Klaus Wagenbach, *Franz Kafka, Années de jeunesse* (1883–1912), Paris: Mercure, 1967.

[16] Deleuze and Guattari, *Kafka*, 20.

[17] Deleuze and Guattari, *Ibid*, 16.

(with intended extermination, to wit "Welsh Not") at the hands of the *other*, and also a second language in which they perform to their global constituency. The shift from one language to another is never a case of translation: "to translate songs is a bastard", says singer Gruff Rhys, whose often use of words for their sound rather than poetic logic would be undermined by the conventional process of translation where "rhymes are usually lost. Replaced by an awkward gaggle of uncomplimentary words."[18] The address of their constituency through the medium of English, however, and no doubt inevitably, does not preclude the writing of songs in Welsh, songs that are usually reserved for extended play release accompanying English-language A-sides—but with the notable exception of the 2000 long play *Mwng*.[19] Commenting specifically on the "impossibility" of translation by reference to the songs on the *Mwng* album, Gruff Rhys nonetheless submits "dumb and humble" English versions of the song lyrics for visitors to the album's website, charging the reader/listener to "burn all your linguaphone tapes and enjoy the stereo bilingual experience that is *Mwng*".[20] One among these songs is, arguably, a condensation of the ground that is prerequisite to critical cultural engagement today:

> [...] they say we're peripheral people
> Spineless and feeble
> Roughneck and evil
> [...] it's so cool in the eye of the fountain
> But the peripheries sustain
> The hottest nettle
>
> Joining the periphery
> Banished to the periphery
> To join the periphery
> The price to pay for all who stray
>
> [...] there's talk of the demon in music
> That divides and rules us
> In musical envy
> [...] it's so lonely on the periphery
> As if looking from afar

---

[18] Mwng website, www.mwng.co.uk/mwnglyrics, accessed 16 November 2006.

[19] The album Mwng, released in 2000, is "an unapologetic assumption that fans of the album would not find Welsh an insurmountable obstacle to the enjoyment of the music. And why should they? Since at least 1986 music fans have embraced musics of cultures generally considered "foreign" [...] This boils down ... to that issue of (post-colonial) power." Griffiths and Hill, "Postcolonial Music", 229.

[20] Mwng website, www.mwng.co.uk/mwnglyrics, accessed 16 November 2006.

At something that's near[21]

The periphery, since poststructuralism, has been consistently the internal site of exteriority, the "outside" from which alterity becomes imaginable. The words to "Ymaelodi Â'r Ymylon" invoke the Welsh idiomatic and divisive "demon in music" that for SFA impacts on their "experiences of doing taboo moves like singing in English … being banished from a [Welsh-language] musical scene".[22] Of course, the same expulsion potentially awaits when the band deliberately opts to sing in Welsh to a non-conversant constituency, as it usually does at least once in such performances (and as it not infrequently does on its English-language releases), when expulsion would be from an English-language music scene. The periphery in question has consequently been described as double-sided, "the periphery of Anglo-American popular culture, and the periphery of Welsh musical culture",[23] the *in-between* or "third" space variously invoked in the cultural theory of the past few decades in resistance to the "politics of polarity".[24]

But it is in their English-language output, without question, that SFA are most able to exercise a sustained political radicalness because, despite any intention to the contrary, everything in linguistic minorisation is political.[25] For Deleuze and Guattari, the notion of a minor literature takes shape around the theoretical deterritorialisation of the major language. The poet Dylan Thomas, for instance, is instructive in this respect, a religiously nonconformist Welshman (and, though we tend to forget it, native Welsh speaker) writing in English, demonstrating how a minor language (that is Thomas's *minorisation* of English, his variant within the standard dialect—not the Welsh language, therefore) plays its part not only in keeping the major language (that is standard English) alive, but also in invigorating and making the major language exhilarating in the ongoing process:

> The minor "treatment" of a major language must be understood in the medical sense of the term. This is obviously the case in the literary treatment—but this is also the case of the treatment through minor dialects and registers. English literature, as is well known, is peopled by Scots, the Irish and the Welsh: *Under*

---

[21] SFA, "Ymaelodi Â'r Ymylon" ("Joining the Periphery" or "Banished to the Periphery").

[22] Mwng website, www.mwng.co.uk/mwnglyrics, accessed 16 November 2006.

[23] Griffiths and Hill, "Postcolonial Music", 229.

[24] Homi K. Bhabha, *The Location of Culture*, 38–9.

[25] Deleuze and Guattari, *Kafka*, 17.

Milk Wood is an example of an extraordinary minorisation of English—it is through such minorisation that the language lives.[26]

Beyond this, however, deterritorialisation marks a disruption to the dominant that distinguishes the linguistic from the political, for instance, to the extent that *linguistic* domination destabilises the normally unproblematic *political* relation between victor and vanquished, proposing as it then does instances of inversion where the language of the vanquished comes to dominate the language of the victor.[27] It is as a consequence that minorisation in these terms is argued as being both directly political and collective when "the people" speak, but the same argument immediately balks at the irresistible tendency of the dominant towards hegemony, even towards imperialism,

> [in] its extraordinary capacity for being twisted and shattered and for secretly putting itself in the service of minorities who work it from inside, involuntarily, unofficially, nibbling away at that hegemony as it extends itself: the reverse of power.[28]

Under the conditions of this reversal, it is the minority's false consciousness that both binds and blinds it to its own absorption by the hegemonic dominant, whose expansion overtakes any capacity effectively and critically to engage with and subvert it.

Take the turtle and hare

So any claim to belong to, or to speak for, a minority achieves very rapid redundancy: *minorisation*, on the other hand, submits active change through the dominant medium. Forget subliminal messaging or backmasking—Dylan Thomas had that clever little move nailed twenty years before "Stairway to Heaven", when he guided his listeners along the streets and in through the out doors of Llareggub[29]—rather to subject language to new forces that come at it from the "outside", or that rise out of holey space, out of the earth turned into swiss cheese,[30] destabilising, disorienting, *rewriting* and invigorating language in the process. When SFA think in one language and write in another, some

---

[26] Jean-Jacques Lecercle, *Deleuze and Language*, 197.

[27] Years spent reading the Latin element in the Welsh language under the tutelage of the great Professor D. Simon Evans taught me as much.

[28] Deleuze and Parnet, *Dialogues*, 58.

[29] Not in the same "evil" league, perhaps, as the claims made for the Led Zeppelin classic, but censorious editors quickly intervened to alter the town's name from Llareggub to Llaregyb when *Under Milk Wood* was first published in 1954 (Thomas was helpless to resist; he died in 1953).

[30] Deleuze and Guattari, *A Thousand Plateaus*, 413.

inspired collisions set your teeth on edge: "Moog Droog", "Glô in the dark", "Pam V".[31] When they sing in an accent not previously heard on Anglo-American frequencies, the listener stops and looks, and critically at that point what SFA do takes on a collective value. Active but not participant in the dominant culture and language, the music of SFA results from the productive context of the dominant where, Deleuze and Guattari observe, "there are no possibilities for an individual enunciation", and, as by default, every enunciation will refer to a collectivity.[32] First the connection of the individual to a political immediacy; second the deterritorialisation of language; and third the collective assemblage of enunciation, all together combine to give us the characteristics of minor literature as outlined by Deleuze and Guattari in the Kafka book. Though part critical of Deleuze and Guattari's only surface analysis of the politics of culture, David Lloyd (writing on nationalism and minor literature) nonetheless indicates the value of the theory, which is to recognise

> the prior emergence of a combative field of literature that is expressly political insofar as the literature … of "minorities" or formerly marginalised communities, calls into question the hegemony of central cultural values. A retrospective, even belated, analysis discovers in articulating the political structure of the canon the terms of an aesthetic culture that have already been negated by a new literature.[33]

Negation of the established culture through minorisation therefore makes minor literature political at the point of enunciation, antiauthoritarian to the degree that it has the effect of opening up a space in which voices that otherwise escape the totalising formulations of formalist organisation now become audible.[34]

There is the contention, of course, that although "minor" in Deleuze and Guattari's sense, minor literature always circulates within the reigning hermeneutic as simply one kind of literature among others in the dominant language. It might be suggested that in privileging particular instances in their discussion (such instances as Kafka), Deleuze and Guattari introduce a *privileged double* to combat a reactionary or reterritorialising major literature, and in so doing they "privilege only a certain kind of minor literature … [which] the major language or canonical critical codes can misrecognise as major

---

[31] Operative in both languages, such examples in song titles inevitably work best for those who are conversant in both and who can therefore participate in the collision; "Moog Droog", for instance, incorporates Robert Moog of music synthesizer fame, but also submits a variant on the English "wacky backy" that only the bilingual listener is likely to be attuned to.

[32] Deleuze and Guattari, *Kafka*, 17.

[33] David Lloyd, *Nationalism and Minor Literature*, 5.

[34] Louis A. Renza, "A White Heron", 27.

according to their own standards".[35] As a result of that misrecognition, the so-called minor literature loses its specificity. Responding to this bone, however, we should recognise that Deleuze and Guattari make at least strategic use of Kafka for a reevaluation of the criteria used to define "literature"; and in reactivating Kafka's work and authority in the name of minor literature, after its critical neutralising through cooption into the dominant literary canon, rather than reinforcing the established system the effect is to make visible the boundaries and limits of the same. Such delineation and mapping of the system then make possible its negotiation and potential breaching, so investing the minor with political function and exposing the dominant's ideological operation and its "ways of making you think".[36] Lloyd is again instructive, describing how the stakes here go beyond different conceptions of subjectivity or redefined literary genres, to foreground the historical and political motives of minorisation:

> a minor literature pushes further the recognition of the disintegration of the individual subject of the bourgeois state, questioning the principles of originality and autonomy that underwrite that conception of the subject.[37]

To reiterate (a) the individual's political immediacy, (b) the deterritorialisation of language and (c) the collectivity of utterance as Deleuze and Guattari's criteria for minor literature; integration of the criteria in the literary matter submitted as minor now gives us occasion to analyse what is played out in the texts themselves: "since the language is arid," they charge, "make it vibrate with a new intensity".[38]

Acting upon this impulse becomes possible in a cultural moment when existing, established value systems fail sufficiently to impose themselves—and that very failure results not only because of the changing culture, but also because of the disintegration of the institutional structures that once presented culture as eternal. Deleuze and Guattari append to Kafka the Irish minor literary variant demonstrated in Joyce's use of English and of every language, and in Beckett's use of English and of French, "but the former [English] never stops operating by exhilaration and overdetermination and brings about all sorts of worldwide reterritorialisations".[39] Minor literatures emerge from the silence that oppressed people and entire cultures were formerly reduced to, and as such they are practical manifestations of once unheard voices. Becoming audible, they relate not merely previously oppressed states, but past, present and future

---

[35] Louis A. Renza, *Ibid*, 34.
[36] SFA, "Hermann Loves Pauline".
[37] David Lloyd, *Nationalism and Minor Literature*, 25.
[38] Deleuze and Guattari, *Kafka*, 19.
[39] Deleuze and Guattari, *Ibid*, 19.

differences—and specifically the difference between the identity that would be imposed upon them and the identity they would choose for themselves.[40] SFA affirm:

> It's not where you're from
> It's not where you're at
> It's not where you've been
> It's where you're between
> It's not what you've been
> It's not what you've seen
> It's where you're between
> […]
>
> From A to Bee
> Then onto Cee
> Don't stop the journey
> 'Til you get to Zee
> 'Til you get to Zee
> There's nothing to see
> Don't stop the journey
> […] [41]

In-betweens proliferate, interstices and passages between stable points are where language no longer needs to function as representative, precisely so that it can now *"move toward its extremities or its limits"* and manifest resistance to the exercise (through language) of power.[42] Bedded in the vernacular, the then vehicular travel of English as an urban if not global language of government, commerce and bureaucracy now splinters into a referential language of sense and culture, ultimately working through the holes to its mythic form on the horizon of cultures. Citing Henri Gobard's tetralinguistic model, Deleuze and Guattari draw the distinctions between each: "vernacular language is *here*; vehicular language is *everywhere*; referential language is *over there*; mythic language is *beyond*".[43]

Don't run around when you can walk there

SFA roam the English language in their music as the nomad moves through smooth space without restriction or directive, boring into the "swiss cheese" of

---

[40] see note 7.
[41] SFA, "The International Language of Screaming".
[42] Deleuze and Guattari, *Kafka*, 23. Emphasis in original.
[43] Deleuze and Guattari, *Ibid*, 23.

the vehicular and surfacing in the referential: "Move you / Buy and sell you / Terrorise you / Mass destruct you / Flaunt you / Disconnect you / Cluster fuck you / We will crush you".[44] If we choose to do so, we can decode the references, but perhaps even to *say* as much is already to have said too much in the face of densely accumulated imagery. Rational, objective engagement with language becomes dismissive of its performance—the productive alternative is to enter into a relationship with the words themselves in their musical articulation, to establish new premises, to decode the irrational instead of attempting to decipher the rational. The sense in sequential images of disintegration emerges, potentially, in our sharing of SFA's metaphor of unplugged information technology, from which arises the "polyphony" once described by no less than Jacques Lacan: "there is in effect no signifying chain that does not have, as if attached to the punctuation of each of its units, a whole articulation of relevant contexts suspended "vertically", as it were, from that point".[45] SFA pick up and strum their acoustic Flying Vs, singing and screaming:

And we
Live together under
Fantasy
Oak trees
In the dark
We make sparks
So unique
We're the mountain people

[...]

Because
They don't care about
You and me
Obviously
Hand-me-down
Culture
Waiting for the vulture
Yes-yes-yes
We're the mountain people

Hibernation comes so early
This year
Dig the peat
Pile it high

---

[44] SFA, "Slow Life".
[45] Jacques Lacan, *Écrits*, 154.

Let it dry
One last chance at ignorance
No fat chance
We're the mountain people[46]

Riding the scree, the mountain people deterritorialise in the most literal terms as expression is infused with metaphor and subjective irrationality, overtaking the otherwise rational expression that is philosophical. Those who inhabit the range are charged by Deleuze and Guattari to "transpierce the mountains instead of scaling them, excavate the land instead of striating it, bore holes in space instead of keeping it smooth, turn the earth into swiss cheese"[47] as they carve out, through holey holes, the holey space of their movement and emergence. The English language (it was suggested in 1975—a lot has changed since then, though not as much as we might like to think) "has become the worldwide vehicular language";[48] their minor deployment within the dominant makes SFA distinctly *more* than passengers. Critically, the variant carries political implication as we are reminded that "there is nothing that is major or *revolutionary* except the minor",[49] and so understood the voice that sings senses itself a stranger within its own language. Whichever language it may be— English, Welsh, German, Yiddish, Czech—the language is always a mixture,

> a schizophrenic mélange ... in which very different functions of language and distinct centres of power are played out, blurring what can be said and what can't be said; one function will be played off against the other, all the degrees of territoriality and relative deterritorialisation will be played out.[50]

Minorisation concedes always to the dominance of the dominant, to the extent that destruction of the vehicular is never its objective. Rather, what the minor variant does is to make possible effective critical dissent *and departure from* the dominant, whereby the latter remains necessarily intact, but its continued domination now becomes virtual instead of actual. Though the feeling of impotence and paralysis may be overwhelming for the individual who gradually realises the enveloping presence of the dominant and the "unintelligible power of circumstances",[51] reality apprehended is simultaneously fractured. Kafka's Josef K., we once read, thought of flies as he was led to execution, their tiny

---

[46] SFA, "Mountain People".
[47] Deleuze and Guattari, *A Thousand Plateaus*, 413.
[48] Deleuze and Guattari, *Kafka*, 24.
[49] Deleuze and Guattari, *Ibid*, 26. My emphasis.
[50] Deleuze and Guattari, *Ibid*, 26.
[51] Georg Lukács, "The Ideology of Modernism", 155.

limbs breaking as they struggled away from the fly-paper;[52] now, question SFA, "when the insects fly all around you / do you reach and aim a hit / or do you lie around [...]?"[53] The second alternative offers nothing and ceases to be an option for SFA, as their musical medium—emphatically—takes over:

> Every time I look around me everything seems so stationary
> It just sends me the impulse to become reactionary
> Spell it out, rip it up, rearrange it, on the contrary
> If I scream it I mean it, I hope you will understand me
> [...].[54]

References

Bhabha, Homi K. *The Location of Culture*. London and New York: Routledge, 1994.

Deleuze, Gilles and Guattari, Félix. *A Thousand Plateaus: Capitalism and Schizophrenia*. Trans. Brian Massumi. Minneapolis: University of Minnesota Press, 1987.

———. *Kafka: Toward a Minor Literature*. Trans. Dana Polan. Minneapolis: University of Minnesota Press, 1986.

Deleuze, Gilles and Parnet, Claire. *Dialogues*. Trans. Hugh Tomlinson and Barbara Habberjam. New York: Columbia University Press, 1987.

Griffiths, Dai and Hill, Sarah. "Postcolonial Music in Contemporary Wales: Hybrids and Weird Geographies." In *Postcolonial Wales*, edited by Jane Aaron and Chris Williams. Cardiff: University of Wales Press, 2005.

Kafka, Franz. *The Trial*. Trans. Idris Parry. London: Penguin, 2000.

Lacan, Jacques. *Écrits: A Selection*. Trans. Alan Sheridan. London: Routledge, 1977.

Lecercle, Jean-Jacques. *Deleuze and Language*. Basingstoke and New York: Palgrave Macmillan, 2002.

Lloyd, David. *Nationalism and Minor Literature: James Clarence Mangan and the Emergence of Irish Cultural Nationalism*. Berkeley: University of California Press, 1987.

Lukács, Georg. "The Ideology of Modernism" (1957). In *Marxist Literary Theory: a Reader,* edited by Terry and Drew Milne. Oxford: Blackwell, 1996.

---

[52] Franz Kafka, *The Trial*, 175: "He was reminded of flies wrenching their legs off in the struggle to free themselves from fly-paper."

[53] SFA, "If You Don't Want Me to Destroy You".

[54] SFA, "The International Language of Screaming".

Pasolini, Pier Paolo. "Grenneriello." In *Lutheran Letters,* trans. Stuart Hood. Manchester: Carcanet Mill Press, and Dublin: Raven Art Press, 1983.

Renza, Louis A. *"A White Heron" and the Question of Minor Literature.* Madison: University of Wisconsin Press, 1984.

Super Furry Animals. "If You Don't Want Me To Destroy You." In *Fuzzy Logic.* Creation Records CRECD190, 1996.

———. "The Man Don't Give a Fuck." In *The Man Don't Give a Fuck.* Creation Records CRESCD, 1996.

———. "The International Language of Screaming." In *Radiator.* Creation Records CRELP214, 1997.

———. "Herman Loves Pauline." In *Radiator.* Creation Records CRELP214, 1997.

———. "Mountain People." In *Radiator.* Creation Records CRELP214, 1997.

———. "Ymaelodi Â'r Ymylon." In *Mwng.* Placid Casual PLC03CD, 2000.

———. "Venus and Serena." In *Phantom Power.* Sony B00009RA99, 2003.

———. "Slow Life." In *Phantom Power.* Sony B00009RA99, 2003.

Tzara, Tristan. *Seven Dada Manifestos and Lampisteries.* Trans. Barbara Wright. London: Calder, 1992.

Williams, Raymond. *Politics and Letters: Interviews with New Left Review.* London: New Left Books, 1979.

Chapter Two

On Community, Institutions and Politics in the Life and Work of Robert Erickson

John MacKay

Abstract: The role of Robert Erickson in North American new music is seminal. He does not have the celebrity status of other (eminently worthy) individuals such as John Cage, Edgard Varèse, Elliot Carter, Milton Babbitt or Steve Reich, to name only a few. John MacKay impresses upon the reader in this essay that Erickson was a tireless worker, a talented innovator and composer as well as a committed and passionate teacher of new music, especially during that explosive period of the 1960s and 1970s in California. What emerges in this biographical sketch, of which MacKay is a part, is a configuration that brings together the significant elements in the personal, social, musical and political-institutional life that touched Erickson, all of which is designated, "community". There is here no imposed dialectic; rather, the author offers a take on a series of events, delicately and succinctly drawn, that trace out multiple patterns of development, or *formation,* operating at both a personal and collective level. The figure of Erickson is like a cipher: he immersed himself in philosophical discourse and that of physics, yet rejected the academicism of "professional literary musicology"; he was influenced by the rigours of Ernst Krenek's methodologies, yet wrote performance-based satiric new music theatre; he embraced so-called world music, collaborated with engineers in instrumental innovation, and negotiated the politics of institutional life without compromising the relationship with music, students and friends. MacKay's conclusion is that through a mix personal qualities that allowed this deeply introspective man to participate collectively without greed, rancour or alienation, Erickson embodies a radical politics, one of permanent, undogmatic, perhaps democratic revolution.

There is much to write about on composer Bob Erickson's status as an American experimentalist. Of particular interest is the symbiotic relationship between his writings and his music and the apparent personal mixture of phenomenology and the cognitive and *Gestalt* sciences which informed his thinking. The prospect of writing about Erickson's unique sense of community and politics, however, is an exciting one. To write about Bob Erickson is for this writer to return to a personal well-spring; for those fortunate enough to know him, Erickson has never ceased to enlighten and inspire. In this paper I recount some of the significant events in Erickson's life with the aim of elaborating the rudiments of a sociology, or even ethnology, of the composer's embeddedness in society.

For musicians, especially composers, the concept of "community" is clear. It is defined in questions of: Who composes? Who listens? Who plays? Who writes about music? Who organizes music? Who leads? Who follows? Who supports? And perhaps most importantly, Who pays? These questions define a community, the necessary role of institutions and ultimately the politics of a particular kind of music. Yet, as surely as a community creates music, music creates community; artists intuitively, willfully and by necessity accept relationships with a set of practical circumstances which profoundly influences, and even determines, their music. In the remarkable case of Robert Erickson, the composer has plotted not only an intriguing and historically significant course among these bedrock cultural issues, but in so doing has graced us with a wealth of personal, anecdotal and ultimately musical commentary on the subject. John Rockwell provides a valuable frame for Erickson's significance in the American context as well as an insightful point of departure for this discussion:

> Now, however, there is a countercurrent at work, a newly fashionable mind-set that seeks to revitalize individual and regional independence and to assert the value of work and lives that don't easily subscribe to dominant mores as propagated from the old cultural capital (New York), or the new one (Los Angeles) ... Robert Erickson's career has epitomized that movement in the realm of serious contemporary composition. Like so many Northern Californians, he came from somewhere else. Yet his arrival there in 1953 must have seemed like coming home. Immediately, he plunged into activities that helped define a scene, not so much as a "school" of like-minded composers and their student epigones, but as a playing field for activity in which individuality could flourish. He did that by example as a composer; as a teacher at the San Francisco Conservatory and the University of California at Berkeley and later at the University of California at San Diego, whose music department for a while functioned as a curious southern outpost of the San Francisco sensibility; and as an administrator, at KPFA radio in Berkeley and at the San Francisco Tape Music Center.[1]

Clearly however, other factors had already played heavily upon Erickson's outlook and attitudes prior to his move to California; among these Erickson cites the years at Park House in the late 1930s, work in the Army as a recruitment officer and the friends he met there, and the highly formative teacher-mentor experience with renown composer, Ernst Krenek. At the beginning of Erickson's odyssey, having left home in the classical manner of the times, to study and make a living in the big city, in this case, Chicago, Erickson was

---

[1] Charles Shere, *Thinking Sound Music*, ix-x

fortunate enough to get work at a music publishing house at which he made his initial contacts with the diaspora of the Second Viennese School:

> There were no textbooks or introductions to study—only the music itself. I had gotten a job at the Gamble Hinged Music Company, so we were able to acquire some of the music of Schoenberg, Berg and Webern from abroad. I remember how puzzled I was by some of the passages in Schoenberg's *opus 33a* for piano. Try as I would I could not make those places correspond to such descriptions of the technique as I found in Marion Bauer's book or the article by Erwin Stein in *Modern Music*. George was deeply involved in an analysis of Berg's *Lyric Suite*, and all of us soon became interested in Berg's *Violin Concerto*[2].

The "we" of the excerpt were Ben Weber and George Perle—all were colleagues in counterpoint with Wesley La Violette at Park House, which at the time was a remarkable "speak-easy" venue for progressive thought on the Chicago Gold Coast. This environment became a new home for Erickson, where he met and married his lifelong companion, painter Lenore Alt. It was here also that Erickson developed a passion for what Rockwell terms "scenes" above "schools":

> About a dozen people lived there; a hundred or more came there regularly. There were interest groups—music, dance, drama, books, arts folk-dance—which met weekly, and on Fridays there was always a large gathering with dinner and a speaker. Park House had elements of a club, a settlement house, a large family, a church, and what we now would call a commune. I felt close to a group of people for the first time in my life, and I had a chance to talk to people with well-stocked minds ... I was the youngest person there, nineteen, ready to talk, argue and harangue—so exhilarated by ideas, art, music, dance, friends, communal feeling, that during the day, delivering samples for the Bradner-Smith Paper Company, I sometimes felt I was dancing along above the pavement.[3]

The Second World War, Park House and the growing contact with the music of Schoenberg, Berg, Webern and Krenek inevitably fostered important socially as well as musically political outlooks for the young composer, including a keen awareness of the destructive esthetics of fascism and by contrast, his own dedication to pedagogical integrity and personal craft and expression. It is interesting that in Erickson's reflections on the military in the 1940s [4], we see only generous commentary on the rich spectrum of people and personalities he

---

[2] Robert Erickson, "Hearing Things" 17. The contact with the Second Viennese School was largely through Krenek, but Erickson recounts a very interesting lesson with Schoenberg in 1939 passing through at the State University in Ypsilanti Michigan. Robert Erickson, *Ibid*, 18.

[3] Robert Erickson, *Ibid*, 15.

[4] Robert Erickson, *Ibid*, chapter 4.

encountered; any criticism of the "military industrial complex" seems to be masterfully shaded into compositions of the late 1960s. During his time as a conscript, Erickson developed a close personal friendship with Aaron Dorsky, an old, wizened businessman who would enliven his interest in organizations— "how they worked and didn't work." For Dorsky's part, he certainly must have valued the warm clarity and buoyancy of the young composer's outlook.[5] The relationship with Krenek, while perhaps less personal, was a powerful and enduring meeting of minds initiated by the young Erickson's inquiring letters on the subject of Krenek's book, *Music Here and Now*. The relationship with Krenek would later draw Erickson and his wife, Lenore Alt, out of their wartime reclusiveness—making ceramics in Michigan—to flourish with him at Hamline, St. Paul, until Krenek's sudden departure for the Southwest in June of 1947.[6] While Krenek's departure left a void for Erickson, he and Lenore stayed on in St. Paul to enjoy at least for a few years the relative security a first academic appointment before the inevitable departure for California in 1953.[7] Krenek's influence, however, followed Erickson into the upper realms of academia, especially in the form of Erickson's first published book, *Sound Structure of Music*.[8] The influence of Krenek must surely have helped open doors at University of California, Berkeley. Much later it was Krenek's definitive recommendation that brought Erickson to University of California, San Diego as a founding professor of their new Department of Music.

Given that they were relative outsiders to the Bay Area, Bob and Lenore's entry into the thick of things was, not surprisingly, quick and graceful. Bob immediately joined and became active in the Bay Area Composer's Forum. He also managed part-time teaching appointments at San Francisco State University where he attracted Pauline Oliveros and Loren Rush as private students. Only a year after arriving, Erickson applied and was accepted as the new music director of the Pacifica Foundation's KPFA, where he found himself at the heart of intense local and even international political-artistic activity:

---

[5] Robert Erickson, *Ibid*, 45.

[6] Erickson cites many important friendships from this time with Robert Holiday, Glenn Glasow, Tom Nee, Will Ogdon. Erickson valued their easy-going qualities of openness and directness as well as their consummate musicianship. At Hamline, a family atmosphere pervaded, fostered by Krenek's intense but very collegial direction of studies. Robert Erickson, *Ibid*, 24.

[7] Charles Shere, *Thinking Sound Music*, 26. Shere also comments on the general scene in Minnesota which Krenek was developing with Dmitri Mitropolus as conductor of the Minnesota Symphony. See also Robert Erickson, "Hearing Things," 27.

[8] Erickson, a formidable student, and omnivorous reader from an early age, gave full testament to Krenek's pedagogical legacy in his highly successful and strikingly pan-historical study of counterpoint, *The Structure of Music: A Listener's Guide*.

My experience at KPFA was intensely sociological and political—the politics of small groups. The day after I started work the assembly exploded at its bi-annual meeting and a large group resigned, many of them KPFA staff members ... Power struggles, factionalism, and ideological controversy were a part of life at the station, and more and more an interesting part of it.[9]

Erickson persisted with KPFA through the rough but exciting years to follow, accepting a position on the board in 1955 and hand-picking subsequent music directors, until he resigned from the Foundation in 1963.

In the position at UC Berkeley, which he held from 1955 to 1957, Erickson was thrust into a political situation that involved a protracted, no-win turf war with very a significant regime of "professional literary musicologists," a struggle he had no trouble leaving for the more engaging and musically substantial environment of the San Francisco Conservatory. The issues however, of "literary professionalism" and later, of all impractically abstract studies of music were enduring objects of Erickson's critical instincts. As he would write much later in 1983:

What started as a mild infection indigenous to the European art wars has been transmitted to the American academy, where specious explanation and systematic theory construction are now out of control. A flood of dissertations and journal papers are spewing out of our graduate schools, written all too often by those who are neither able to perform nor compose music, nor (judging from the writing) able to hear it. The academic wave of the future may turn out to be the wave of the musically deaf.[10]

It is not hard to see how closeness to sound would become one of the guiding polemics of Erickson's compositional and scholarly outlook. But Erickson was also quick to see the evolving tyranny of complexity and abstraction in any musical discipline. For Erickson, the significance of sound and not the formulations of composers, theorists and musicologists was the ultimate judge of all things musical—a point of view which was at once liberating as it was demanding in new and different ways.

Not unlike New York's "downtown" (versus "uptown") scene, The San Francisco Conservatory and the offshoot of the San Francisco Tape Music Center created very serious countercurrents to academic composition in the early 1960s. Erickson's presence as a senior figure played catalytically among a remarkable and diverse collection of stars including Terry Riley, Pauline Oliveros, Morton Subotnick, Ramon Sender and Loren Rush, witnessing the historic births and rebirths of music theatre, minimalism, improvisation, live electronics, multimedia and the exciting although ultimately transient

---

[9] Robert Erickson, "Hearing Things," 53.
[10] Robert Erickson, "Hearing Things," 4.

phenomenon of a community of experimental musicians and researchers. The issue of the academic versus "secular" composer [11] continued thematically in Erickson's work, as, of course, he belonged to both camps; an omnivorous reader, his regime of personal research in this period produced remarkable studies of Archytas and Bergsonian temporality in music, some of his most intricate and challenging compositions as well as a Guggenheim Fellowship for research in Sweden and Poland in 1966.[12]

The opportunity of founding the new Department at University of California, San Diego was mutually beneficial for both the institution and the composer. As John Stewart would remark, Erickson was a necessary ingredient of "legitimacy" for the new and experimental school.[13] Although Erickson was deeply satisfied with his work in San Francisco, the original collective was fracturing and the new appointment gave him the opportunity to work in a major institution on experimental research and, with the help of longtime friend Will Ogdon, to design a department from the ground up:

> We wanted to make a rather different music department, one with a lot of daily contact between teachers and students, but without the usual packaging into degrees, units, grades and other trivia. We wanted to make a place where composers and performers could work in tandem to produce fine performances of contemporary and other music, where the making and performing of music was a central activity, and where research and theory could reflect twentieth century concerns. Music teaching in American institutions has always been conservative. Conservatories are the worst, for conservatory teachers train their students to meet market demands, and they seldom stray far from the repertory of concert hall favorites. Musicology is well established in American universities, but rarely do musicologists work in the field of contemporary music, preferring the respectable past. Their work has been chiefly literary research: deciphering of manuscripts, making editions, scholarly debates over the details of long past artistic controversies. We wanted to try to initiate other kinds of research, and to draw on methodologies from disciplines such as linguistics, physics, and psychology, in the hope that different approaches might help to illuminate new and old musical problems.[14]

Whether the new department became a "San Francisco South" or an "Illinois

[11] Morton Subotnick's phrase. See Robert Erickson, "Hearing Things," 65.

[12] Robert Erickson, "The Musical System of Arcytas," *ex tempore* VI/2 (Summer 1993): 79-98. See also "Hearing Things," ch. 7, and Erickson, "Time Relations," *Journal of Music Theory* 7 (Winter 1963): 174-192.

[13] Forum comments in the "Erickson Celebration" at UCSD in January of 1987.

[14] Robert Erickson, "Hearing Things," 147.

West"[15] experimentalism flourished, courses were offered, which were unthinkable in any environment outside of UC San Diego, and the school quickly acquired the profile of one of the, if not *the,* experimental new music centers on the West Coast. Empowered and perhaps even inspired by the institutional security, Erickson's work branched out in many dialects of rigorous experimentation. He collaborated with cutting-edge virtuosi such as bassist, Bertram Turetzky, and trombonist, Stuart Dempster—and later percussionists, Ron George and Dan Dunbar and trumpeter, Ed Harkins. In the context of personal explorations in world music—Erickson spent the summer of 1974 in Bali and Indonesia—Erickson involved himself in instrument building with local aerospace and acoustic engineer, Ed Hujsak. At the same time, Erickson conducted an ongoing, uniquely musical-scientific examination of "timbre", which would lead to his second book, *Sound Structure in Music* published in 1975.

The musical pieces of the late 1960s, which sprang from these progressive, even anti-establishment research interests, were rich in communal spirit and, often, not surprisingly, laced with political innuendo. *Down at Piraeus,* for soloist, chorus and tape takes on an excerpt of Plato's *Republic,* Book III, which extols the manly and belligerent virtues of the Dorian and Phrygian modes, thus making, in a melodic style speculative of the ancient scalic systems, "a mostly rude commentary on Plato's ideas about music [with] a determinedly anti-antiquarian bias," and ending with an interminable harmonic-rhythmic drone on "I believe it", affirming the seeming timelessness of the "might is right" esthetic.[16] *Do It* for speaker, double chorus, gongs, basses and bassoons is distinctly African in extraction, using interlocking syllabic polyrhythms and mixing current advertising slogans in Afro-American dialect (see Example 3-1) with taped snippets from General MacArthur's farewell address and an anti-war poem by Donald Petersen. The remarkable cycling and cataloguing of elements intermingled with the intoxicating speech rhythms forges an unforgettable climax through variations on the term, "power"—RED-uh-POW-UH, YEL-low-POW-UH, POW-UH, LUV a POW UH ("red power," "yellow power," "love of power") to a frightening convergence of the two choruses on POW-WUH in Black protest shouting. The Peterson poem which bears the only semblance of a message in the collage, presents a cynical choice of paying "the two fifty / and that to the right person" to let someone else drop "the bombs and the napalm...."

---

[15] As graduate students in the early 1980s, we would hear the phrase "Illinois West" from people such as Ed Harkins, John Silber, Will Ogdon, and (earlier) Kenneth Gaburo, who were all from the Mid-West, but the San Francisco contingency was just as evident with Pauline Oliveros and frequent visits from Gordon Mumma (UC Santa Cruz), and Morton Subotnick (then at Calarts).

[16] Robert Erickson, "Hearing Things," 150.

and *selling* to that someone else—The name of the game is selling / Be aggressive…." Although, as always, Erickson goes beyond a message, the listener cannot avoid piecing together a very disturbing view of media, privilege, empowerment and aggression.

Example 3-1: Excerpt from beginning of *Do It* 1968 by Robert Erickson. Copyright Sonic Art Editions. Used by permission of Smith Publications, 2617 Gwynndale Ave., Baltimore, MD 21207. (Capitalized syllables are held for two beats and the lower-case syllables for one.)

General Speech (1968) was, by Erickson's own admission, as much Stuart Dempster's invention as his own. Yet the transcription of MacArthur's farewell address (again) for the trombone, complete with gliding inflections, a cough and pauses for a sip of water, in an immaculate cap and uniform with dark glasses and white gloves (designed by Lenore) was as rich a theatrical satire as anything in the period (see Figure 2.) The low, flabby register of the speech, the protracted and virtuosic articulation of the vowels and elaborate rhetorical flailing of the slide comprise a whimsical alternate reality for an icon all too well known in Erickson's generation—even after the lights are dimmed on Dempster's closing pose, the medals and insignia of the costume (etched in florescent paint) glow mysteriously in the dark!

Figure 2: Stuart Dempster performing *General Speech* April 1995, at University of Arizona, Tuscon. Photograph by Russ Widener.

Cardinitas '68 for soprano, five musicians and tape is a piece which marks a direction away from wider audiences and hence toward a more reduced but intimate community, yet without departing from Erickson's typically high level of invention and ingenuity: it was written as a celebration of the first year of the new department for Beverley Ogdon as the soloist.[17] The three original instruments which it requires are the plastic sewer-pipe tube drums, (resined) glove-activated metal rods and the Travertine "chimes" or marimba in tuned marble blocks.[18] The text of the work which Erickson wrote himself is like the music, an open, free-associative, stream of consciousness succession of images and expressions, some rich, and elemental, others seemingly trivial, but all within a long and elegant sense of spiritual journey. The invented sounds of the original instruments carry much of the significance of the piece: the pale and austere purity of the granite chimes, the searing strength and resonance of the metals rods and the rich but somewhat "five-and-dime" *tabla* colorations of the tube drums. What emerges in *Cardinitas '68* is implied in the title, the footprint of a community unique in time and place.

The communal theme of "place" figured prominently in *Pacific Sirens*

---

[17] Cardiff and Encinitas, which comprise the title of the work, are the names of the towns where the Ericksons and Ogdon lived in their first years at UC San Diego.

[18] Erickson is always quick to credit the collaboration of Ed Hujsak, an aerospace engineer and acoustician, who perfected the construction of his instrumental inventions.

(1968) and *Nine and a Half for Henry (and Wilbur and Orville)*, in which ocean surf and urban noise—cars and aeroplanes—are mixed and tuned as quadraphonic environments for ensemble improvisation. Performers with the pitch and timbral elements of their instruments are required to "listen into" the spectral complexes of the environmental noise (the score containing the approximate content of the tape for *Pacific Sirens* appears in Example 3-3) and appropriately blend and protrude. Because of the encounters of the tape sounds (which are filter-tuned to a low F in *Pacific Sirens* and a low F# in *Nine and a Half*) with the instruments, the audience is led to hear anew and recognise the pitched components of environmental sounds. The pieces are remarkably successful in this way; as well as being sensitive explorations of the spectral presence of our natural and industrial surroundings, these pieces clearly point our attention to larger issues of listening and intuitive environmental awareness.

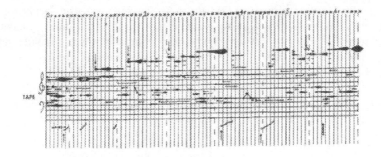

Example 3-2: Score from *Pacific Sirens* 1968 by Robert Erickson.
Copyright Sonic Art Editions. Used by permission of Smith Publications,
2617 Gwynndale Ave., Baltimore, MD 21207.

The sound gathering expedition for *Nine and a Half for Henry (and Wilbur and Orville)* was also the very entertaining subject of a PBS documentary which followed Erickson in his orange jumpsuit, hard hat, tape recorder in hand on freeways, at refineries, up a carillon tower, and to the studio where the sounds were assembled and finally to the recital hall where the ensemble improvised with the tape collage. However, despite the theatrics of the film, both pieces, *Nine and a Half* and *Pacific Sirens* avoid environmentalist commentary in favor of transcendent expressions of sound and community and also, as Erickson would point out later, to the composer's inevitable role in it:

> I really do not compose something until I hear something and it is usually not a musical tune. It is usually some noise or some non-music sound composing the environment in which I live, its sounds, its ambience. At least it has me feeling

that I am here and not someplace else. I am not importing the music from Mars or Europe. It has got its home fingerprints on it. I am charmed by the idea of composing the environment. I don't think of it as composing against the environment, although I guess a lot of composers do compose against it, or in spite of it or never-the-less. [19]

While guiding the growth of the department at UC San Diego was not always smooth sailing, with its share of prima donnas, difficult personalities and administrative drudgery, in the larger scheme of things (which, for Erickson was always in view), it was a winning situation, and, in the end, Erickson could say that "in helping to build a place where composers could feel at home I have built a congenial community for myself."[20] However, a seemingly inevitable turning point was reached along the way, sometime in the in the mid 1970s. Perhaps not coincidentally, after the inaugural concert of the Mandeville Auditorium (to which the Regents were invited), featuring some of the Department's more "ephemeral" work, it was decided that the UC San Diego Music Department should adopt a more serious demeanor and start to graduate (more) students. The direction of the department was temporarily taken over from outside, and generally, closer attention was paid to more goal-directed pursuits in the graduate program.[21] Although this had more of an influence on style over substance, the Department began to function as a music school, and a particularly high profile one for composition with the accompanying elevation of politics, preference and opinion. Erickson wrote the following in 1980:

Until recently I was not aware that students were expected to compose only certain kinds of music—my whole approach to teaching has been to try to help the student find their own way, whatever that might be. I was taken aback during the spring 1983 composition juries to discover that most of our compositional faculty was imposing an esthetic test. Student must not compose repetitive music. One who did, a former student of Stockhausen, was frozen out, not because his music was inept, but because it was the wrong style. I was and am deeply disturbed by this evidence of hardening of the musical arteries, all the more because, when I brought up the point that the faculty was applying a test based on style, there was no sense of alarm, only nodding heads and a murmured "of course." Seed, root, and branch of academicism, all in a phrase and a nod.

This deeply disappointing change of attitude has come about in less than fifteen years, and it has hardened in the last few. It is intimately related to the esthetic loyalties of a group of aging composers. Music in the idioms of composer from

---

[19] "An Interview with Robert Erickson," *Percussive Notes Research Edition* 15/3 (1987): 18.
[20] Robert Erickson, "Hearing Things," 148-150.
[21] The state had earlier scuttled the Departments request for a no-classes, no-grades undergraduate curriculum.

the early and mid-twentieth century are acceptable; roughly speaking, everything through what I think of as "fifties music." Developments since then, particularly exploration that have gone on in contemporary American music, especially music by composers working in repetitive idioms and idioms that seem to appeal to wider audiences, are viewed with disdain or contempt by most of our composers. Wagons are drawn into a circle, guns are loaded for elaborate and tenacious defenses or hard won artistic territory. The music of the evil barbarians must be kept at bay. And new kinds of music can be kept out. It is easy. [22]

Erickson speaks of other instances of academic politics in UC Berkeley, like the shutting out of Arnold Schoenberg from UC Berkeley's celebration of "all" UC composers in the inaugural concert for its new auditorium in the mid-fifties. He complains too of Pierre Boulez's "kidnapping" of Webern at Darmstadt. "The power of the academy to dig in its feet" is awesome," he concludes, and laments, "I am sorry that UC San Diego appears to me to be so fearful of change that it needs to apply Boulez's sort of esthetic test to our young composers, all the more, because, if anything at all is certain, it is that what is current will fade into the past as the new comes into being." What Erickson wanted most was for "our students to understand the world beyond the university, and how to exist in it. Music of any consequence should be for people and organizations beyond the classroom. I see our department as very much a halfway house to the outside world."[23]

But change itself will change and further transformations of the Department would leave Erickson even more on the periphery in relation to the dramatic rise of the Center for Music Experiment's Computer Audio Research Laboratory via a huge grant from Systems Development Corporation in the early 1980s:

We are changing at UC San Diego into a hi tech wonderland, flooded with students who are good at math and terrible at reading, thinking or hearing music. Computer types (wrong sort) obsessed with typing in the perfect algorithm for the ultimate intellectual construction. They are not much concerned with how the result sounds—it is sort of (an) accident, tho all is well if the algorithm is (s)ound. A new kind of program music. So—a certain distance is developing between me and[d] my colleagues. I won't, can't show these budding composers—deafer than Beethoven—how to write a modern, up-to-date piece of music. Worse, I want to teach only the ones I think have talent! In the modern university, in the modern world, this is heresy. Everything, absolutely EVERYTHING is supposed to be teachable and learnable. This is a very modern point of view, in tune with our media, civilization, where nothing is presumed to

---

[22] Robert Erickson, "Hearing Things," 152.
[23] Robert Erickson, *Ibid*, 153.

be new, and where talent is equated with remakes of movies, tv shows, even the news .[24]

Holding true to his own advice—"Be in it, not of it!"—Erickson was, at this point, long through with academic politics. Indeed, as he approached retirement age, his day-to-day life was more and more encroached upon by illness, the degenerative myositis,[25] while at the same time his work was attaining long overdue recognition.[26] A remarkable confluence of elements crystallized in Erickson's music in these years. "Drones," "hockets," and "arabesques"[27] appear in all compositions after *Night Music* (1979) in an ever-shifting kaleidoscope of designs and timbral nuance, forging a unique sense of cinematic narrative. The sense of place still pervades—it could seemingly have been written nowhere else—as the luminescent drones resonate with the endless vistas of the Pacific amid the modal microtonality of the arabesques as the freely evolving, sequencing of episodes and colours bespeaks the unhindered natural ease of life of the Southwest. The music is deeply personal, yet at the same time, accessible and intriguing both within the stream of consciousness of individual pieces and between pieces: as one piece finds part of itself in the next, familiar sounds abound but in different story lines, as if in an endless chain of narratives, wherein familiar experiences were replayed from different angles—a kind of personal classicism for all, but especially for a close and immediate following.

Thus while traditional socio-political themes of mentorship, big-city opportunity, and institutional-collegial patronage figure prominently in Erickson's unique odyssey, Rockwell's insight that Erickson was a representative or even prototype of a "countercurrent" moving away from the major cultural centers is significant. However, Rockwell actually understates this case for Erickson, since the immediacy of the music after the mid 1960s seems more and more to be about very specific places and unique circumstances:

> The real America is California. You know what New York magazines and
> newspapers say about California, and you may not understand that the reason

---

[24] From a letter to Charles Shere, cited in *Thinking Sound Music*, 79.

[25] A condition to which Erickson ultimately succumbed in 1996. Throughout the 1970s and 1980s he was already becoming increasingly incapacitated.

[26] Recognition came in the form of various commissions from Betty Freeman and her Whitelight Foundation and an American Institute of the Arts Cash Award.

[27] Drones and hockets were an integral part of Erickson's timbral research up to the mid-seventies. Hockets, as melodies composed of abrupt shifts of isolated tones between instruments, challenge the ear's perception of continuity and drones typically point the ear to and away from the fusion of timbres in static, rich, but harmonically minimal complexes of sound.

they say that is that they too know that the wind is blowing from California towards the East. They may not like it, but that's what it is. So you are the center of the USA. California is one of the places where you can be an outsider still … It is possible not to be a cooperative member of the group if you can stand the isolation. I'm going to follow my whim, I really don't need to be bound … I don't advise anybody to do this—you need to be immune to loneliness, and very few people are.[28]

An inheritor of Krenek's rigorous yet open compositional vistas and of what Shere terms a "principled non-conformity",[29] Erickson's own music underwent one of the most studied and remarkable evolutions of his generation, and in this—over and above the personal commitments, administrative drudgery, the meeting of minds, the butting of heads, cutting of ties—lies his most influential political and intellectual testament: his shift away from traditional classical formal concepts to the improvisation pieces of the early 1960s, world music eclecticism, instrument making, the quasi-political and quasi-environmental pieces, the partnerships in extended instrumental techniques, the timbre / sonority-influenced pieces and research studies, crowned with the uncanny originality and consistency of style over the last 12 years of his work. Remarkably however, there is very little "progressive" development in Erickson's work, where an earlier piece can be seen as directed toward the technique and sophistication of a later piece: to mention only a few favourites, while *Garden* (1977), *Kryl* (1977), *Night Music* (1978), *The Idea of Order at Key West* (1979), *Auroras* (1982), *Sierra* (1984), *Solstice* (1985), and *Corfu* (1986) are of unsurpassed beauty, he certainly wrote no finer pieces than the *Second String Quartet* (1956), *Duo* for violin and piano, (1959), *Concerto for Piano and Seven Instruments, Nick, Mick and the Magees* (1963) for choir, and the *Ricercars* (1966 and 1967) for double bass and tape, and trombone and tape.

Yet if epithets of "freedom of discipline / discipline of freedom" and resolute individualism are to be ascribed to Erickson's creative legacy, he was rarely an outsider anywhere for any great length of time. His great capacity for friendship, gregarious support of public and creative institutions, his easy entrepreneurial spirit of collaboration and the endless agenda of projects and issues of personal research assured a rich, faithful and continuously growing community wherever he was. What he says about California, he ultimately says about himself; namely, that "it is good to feel that my writing is not complete. As long as I am adding ideas, impressions, recovered memories, I can feel that I am in the midst

---

[28] An undated note in a collage of letters on page 12 of the Erickson Celebration program published in 1987 by the Department of Music, UCSD. Charles Shere astutely points out the Emersonian nuance of "whim" in this note. Charles Shere, *Thinking Sound Music*, 70.
[29] Charles Shere, *Ibid*, xvi.

of life, looking outward, oriented in my world, firm in the five directions."[30]

References

Erickson, Robert. *The Structure of Music: A Listener's Guide.* Westport, Connecticut: Greenwood, 1955.

———. "Hearing Things." In *Music of Many Means: Sketches and Essays on the Music of Robert Erickson*, Robert Erickson and John MacKay. Lanham, MD: Scarecrow Press, 1995.

———. "The Musical System of Arcytas." *ex tempore* VI No. 2 (Summer 1993): 79-98

———. "Time Relations." *Journal of Music Theory* 7 (Winter 1963): 174-192.

———. *Sound Structure in Music.* Berkeley: University of California Press, 1975.

Shere, Charles. *Thinking Sound Music: The Life and Work of Robert Erickson.* Berkeley: Fallen Leaf Press, 1995.

---

[30] Robert Erickson, "Hearing Things," 4.

CHAPTER THREE

THE BOWIE BUSINESS: CAPITALISING ON SUBVERSION?

RODNEY SHARKEY

Abstract: This essay addresses the ideas of distance, detachment, experimentation and accessibility in and through the work of David Bowie. Bowie may be seen as a practitioner of metamorphosis in the true Ovidian sense. His artistic output is a song of change, such that his key appeal is that of enigma. Bowie sings of the fluid shifts that take place in a rapidly developing technological society, shifts that the Bowie persona too undergoes as if the singer were a figure in his own theatrical invention, like a street-wise Narcissus. This essay notes the precariousness of attempts to pin down or pigeonhole Bowie's work, and, in so doing, offers a thorough investigation of two ways in which critical discourse consolidates perceptions of rock and roll in relation to capital; namely, strategies of resistance and consumption. Rodney Sharkey notes that Bowie himself was not passive in relation to the theoretical developments that position his work, both in relation to cultural studies and the perceptions of the fans. The kind of transformations undergone by Bowie, themselves correspond to major shifts in theoretical understandings of desire, consumption and culture that occurred during the last quarter of the twentieth century. One of the factors that constitutes Bowie as a central figure in popular culture studies is that he both embodies and contradicts the figure of a socially critical Marxist and equally that of the populist post-Marxian position. Thus to bring any of the various cultural studies frameworks to bear on Bowie is always to be forced into a reflection on the cultural production of theory itself.

Bowie the Artist

It is difficult to evaluate the cultural importance of pop music on its own terms, given that the academic discourse that must necessarily represent it, elides the very factor that makes it popular: its immediate accessibility.[1]

---

[1] David Willis, *Symbolism and Practice*, 11.

By soliciting a range of fan opinion it becomes apparent that to an early fan of his music, David Bowie's principle endearing value was his sheer unpredictability and virtuoso capacity for experimentation. On the other hand, to a current Bowie-netter, such beliefs are an outmoded barometer of his importance.[2] Thus, in response to claims made by early-Bowie fans that his work of the last twenty years is substandard, Bowie-netters reply that this is an accusation that arises because early fans feel betrayed by what they see as Bowie "selling out" to the mainstream in the early nineteen-eighties. In other words, Bowie-netters feel that early Bowie fans' reactions are being governed by an established discourse that equates success with compromising one's music to appeal to a mainstream audience. Concurrently, and as a related and arguably greater sin, early Bowie fans recall the cultural influence of a Bowie who redefined the relationship between rock music and style by becoming self-consciously, self-reflexively stylistic and who introduced a range of other art forms into the chemistry of what was becoming a fairly pedantic musical form. In contrast, they see the Bowie of today as having little or no relevance. Crucially, however, Bowie-netters see Bowie's multi-media performance experimentations in the virtual world of the web as a reiteration and McLuhanesque "extension" of his essential artistic practice. Their argument is that the Internet is the logical step forward for an artist whose career was built on incorporating new technology within a multi-media framework. The inference here for early Bowie fans is that they are old fashioned and out of touch with the effect of technology on art; the very thing that "Space Oddity" (1969)—Bowie's first hit—addressed.

Further, this cyber-space dimension, from the Bowie-netters' point of view, has resulted in Bowie's singularly most admired attribute: his accessibility. For 65 dollars a year, the Bowie-netter can have access to Bowie's on-line journal, provide art design for CD packaging, help select tracks for future CD releases by means of on-line recording sessions, and chat both with Bowie and other members of the Bowie net community. For example, the promotion of *Heathen* (2002) allowed Bowie-netters access to exclusive pre-release listening parties, priority tickets for gigs and even an exclusive Roseland gig, the set list of which was dictated by Bowie-netters through an e-mail vote. According to many such Bowie-netters this unfussy access to Bowie and his work explodes the conventional boundaries imposed by the mythology of the inaccessible rock star and points the way forward for the future of music / fan interaction. In contrast, early Bowie fans baulk at what they perceive to be the deliberate dissolution of

---

[2] This information about Bowie fans was solicited and compiled by talking to a range of early Bowie fans that included multi-media artists, musicians and software providers, and by talking with Bowie-netters in chat-rooms at www.davidbowie.com.

the most painstakingly constructed, stylistically aloof image in rock and roll history. For them, the idea that Bowie is "your mate on the internet" is profoundly disheartening.

Bowie and Discourse

Paul du Noyer: So you'd be very happy if I and another journalist had different ideas of what your songs were about?

David Bowie: Absolutely. As Roland Barthes said in the mid-sixties, that was the way interpretation would start to flow. It would begin with society and culture itself. The author becomes really a trigger.[3]

If one looks closely at the two positions, as outlined in Section I, into which Bowie fans tend to fall, it is clear that they revolve around tropes of distance, resistance, experimentation and subversion on the one hand, and inclusivity, accessibility, intimacy and democracy on the other.

This opposition is interesting because these two views of Bowie are reflections of the two main interpretive discourses in popular culture studies whose genesis and structural development revolve around capital. The first of these discourses has its roots in Adorno's theory of "standardisation" (1991) in which experimentation functions as a resistant response to homogenisation. It was enshrined as the interpretive key for popular culture studies in Dick Hebdige's *Subculture: The Meaning of Style* (1979). Standardisation is the homogenising impulse necessary for capital to maximize profit. It is accomplished through consumer choice limitation which is achieved by the regulation of available consumer product to scarcely competitive alternatives. In popular music this would be the network of producers, studios, record companies and radio stations who, driven by the imperative of profit maximization, work in harmony to predetermine consumer purchase. A classic example of this is the popular radio station, which employs the jingle "hear the hits here first". By working in conjunction with music corporations, sponsors and agents, and by carefully selecting the material broadcast, the radio station plays what will become the hits because competition is strategically delimited. Such hegemony predetermines the successful product to benefit the investment made by the infrastructure in constructing the consumer market. For the consumers, exposed to the same standardised diet, homogenised product becomes the barometer of quality in the given market. However, according to

---

[3] Paul du Noyer, "ChangesFiftyBowie," *Q* Magazine.

Adorno, "serious" and / or experimental music resists this logic.[4] That which does not conform to standards, that which experiments and rebels, rebels against the standardisation of the market both in its refusal to conform and in its provision of a different listening space as an alternative to mass conformity. The first popular culture interpretive discourse employed this logic as first principle of the new discipline.

The second and more recent popular culture discourse is one generated by popular culture theorists who attempt to avoid the pitfalls of a binary opposition polarised in poles of complicity or resistance to capital. This is done by sidestepping the product's relation to capital at the outset of analysis. Moving beyond Adorno, the logic here is that if critical judgement of product is based on capital resistance or complicity then popular culture is "damned before the fact." If all Marx-inspired study of popular culture is tied to identifying and championing product that resists homogenisation then the discourse ignores the interests and concerns of mass culture itself. Essentially, the Adornoesque critic is doing the audience's discerning for them and even politely chastising them from the ivory tower regarding the popular entertainment forms that they consume. As an alternative approach then, this second popular culture studies strain, determined to adapt the essentials of Marxism to its project as a value, indicates its revolutionary principle in the manner of its selection: it moves from consideration and analyses of select (and resistant) elements of the popular, to the most popular itself. In doing this a simultaneous discourse shift takes place

---

[4] By way of example, Adorno suggests that "In [...]serious music the detail virtually contains the whole and leads to the opposition of the whole, while, at the same time, it is produced out of the conception of the whole. In popular music the relationship is fortuitous. The detail has no bearing on the wholes [...] A musical detail which is not permitted to develop becomes a caricature of its own potentialities. Theodor Adorno, "On Popular Music", 7. Adorno finds such development of detail to be a key feature of Beethoven's work and indicative of the type of attention that the serious artists pay to their musical compositions. If, for the sake of argument, we were to consider Peter Buckley's interview with Carlos Alomar regarding the genesis of "Station to Station" in the same terms then one could, using Adorno, suggest that Bowie too was "serious": The opening section was developed from Bowie's ideas by Alomar, who layered and layered more guitar parts and, after a suggestion from Bowie, added arpeggiated figures on guitar as the opening section developed. "The opening is all melody and counterpoint. The rhythm section had already done their stuff and we were watching him with Earl Slick, trying to tell him what was going on: 'I know its long – just keep playing!' He was trying to hold this note for about two minutes for that opening section. And we were saying 'How the hell is he going to hold this note any longer?' 'Plug in another amplifier! Just keep the chain of amplifiers going until the sound keeps going. The feedback we were getting was weird so we just loaded up speakers from room to room to keep it going as long as possible." David Buckley, *Strange Fascination*, 275.

wherein identifying the presence of resistant or subversive tropes is replaced by articulating cultural empowerment. Camille Paglia's treatment of Madonna, *Vamps and Tramps* (1994), is the watershed example wherein the Madonna industry (music, clothing, literature, image) is not examined in terms of exploitation but in terms of her role in empowering women. Paglia's celebratory text demonstrates the shift in critical appraisal away from subversive tropes and towards cultural influence so that resistance is replaced by empowerment and a drive towards establishing an intra-subjective and plural relationship with the body politic.

Bowie and Subjective Preference

For there is nothing either good or bad but thinking makes it so.[5]

In conjunction with these two shifting pop culture metanarratives, the question of legitimation also occupies a prominent place in the mind of the popular culture critic. Simon Frith, the highly respected popular culture theorist, has often acknowledged the difficulty in attempting to side step the issue of personal preference in order to arrive at a working theory of objective value. For example, he writes:

> I'm sure in my own cultural practice that *Jane Eyre* is a better romance than a Mills and Boon or Harlequin title, just as I know that the Pet Shop Boys are a better group than U2 and that Aerosmith has no value at all. The problem is how best to argue this.[6]

In recognising that his own personal value judgement is inextricably bound up with a sense of the intrinsic worth of the artists in question, Frith is confronted with the central dilemma that governs the discipline.[7] When analyzing popular

---

[5] William Shakespeare, *Hamlet,* Act II, Sc. ii, ln 249.

[6] Simon Frith, "Defending Popular Culture from the Populists", 574.

[7] Interestingly, history has a role to play here. Frith wrote the article in question in 1991 when U2 were engaged in a fairly pompous revisionist reading of themselves as the culmination of two hundred years of African-American music. Yet they were to return in 1992 with what is now considered to be the most culturally valuable reassessment of rock and roll legitimacy in a mainstream context. In other words, from an objective point of view, ZOO TV's mega-successful postmodernism outstripped the Pet Shop Boys localised postmodernism by its sheer scale. Further, Frith implicitly acknowledges the role of cultural context in his assessment, by favouring the English band. To an Irish person, U2's successes and failures signify with a far greater cultural resonance than the London-orientated introspections of Neil Tennant, just as Aerosmith may say more to a disaffected and suicidal Sunset Boulevard adolescent than either U2 or the Pet Shop Boys. The implication is that personal preferences are inscribed with a Kantian

culture there is a twin imperative wherein one must interrogate one's own critical position to weed out purely subjective bias *and* simultaneously ratify the importance of the subject matter. By way of contrast, when writing an academic paper on James Joyce one must rigorously examine one's position for critical laziness but one need not be concerned about demonstrating the cultural relevance of the subject matter; James Joyce's cultural importance is a given. In contrast, not only does the pop culture critic have to achieve academic objectivity, he or she also has to use academic discourse to legitimate the importance of the chosen subject as part of the academic exercise. However, this is at once what makes popular culture studies both infuriating and important because this twin imperative is also what allows the popular culture artefact to resonate beyond the limitations of the two primary discourses analyzed in this essay, discourses which essentially govern the discipline. To put it in the simplest terms, popular culture study reveals the degree to which all ostensibly objective value is really determined by subjective preference. When one writes about Joyce one can conveniently ignore that one chose Joyce and not Sartre; both authors occupy seats in the Pantheon. When one writes about Bowie and not Joyce one is immediately obliged to explain "why?" At which point, shorn of subjective preference, intuition and a host of other responses that remain legitimate when the subject matter is enshrined within the academy, the pop culture critic has no armoury other than a critical discourse that legitimates his chosen academic subject. And yet this is what makes popular culture studies unique because the need to legitimate the subject matter renders transparent the representative values of critical discourses that otherwise might be imagined to be objective, authoritative and incontrovertible.

With this in mind, and by way of demonstration, consider the following extremely declarative summary of David Bowie's career between the period 1969 and 1983. It is beyond question that a subjective value judgement is present: David Bowie's early work is better than his later output. In other words, my own subjective preference is now revealed. I believe the music produced by Bowie between 1969 and 1980 to be of more cultural and political relevance than the music that follows it. But as Firth says, "[t]he problem is how best to argue this". What I hope will be of interest in the following argument is the manner in which each of Bowie's signature innovations, and its political repercussions, are articulated by recourse to certain cultural theorists whose writings appear to confirm the value that I imagine inheres in the work in question.

In 1969, David Bowie released an album that rebelled against the principles of liberal humanism that were central to the Woodstock experience; a liberal

---

authenticity that is determined by nothing more than the echo of the listener's own personal and socio-cultural experience.

humanism which appeared at the time to be the only viable political position for a musician with socialist sympathies to adopt. On the album's title track—"Space Oddity"—Bowie had the foresight to recognise that the medium was the message. While the champions of folk music were denouncing technology's encroachment into daily life—typified by the cries of Judas directed at Bob Dylan when he switched to the electric guitar at the Royal Albert Hall [8]—the instrumentation which propels Major Tom's journey into outer space mimics the flight of technology itself; an atonal onomatopoeia reflecting McLuhan's view that

> all media are extensions of some human faculty—psychic or physical. The wheel is an extension of the foot. The book is an extension of the eye. Clothing is an extension of the skin ... electric circuitry, an extension of the central nervous system. Media, by altering the environment, evoke in us unique ratios of sense perceptions. The extension of any one sense alters the way we think and act—the way we perceive the world. When these ratios change, men change.[9]

Despite his great admiration for Bob Dylan as a singer and songwriter, Bowie was not about to reiterate a politics based on a return to pastoral values and its natural rewards. Thus while the motto "All you need is love" desperately tried to drown out the sound of America's involvement in the Vietnam war, Bowie revelled in mechanisation and drew attention to the "love machine that rumbles through desolation rows" in "The Cygnet Committee;" to the "Sun Machine" going down in "Memories of a Free Festival;" and to the spitting cash machines of "God Knows I'm Good." It was not until three years later when Gilles Deleuze and Félix Guattari published the French original of what became known as *Anti-Oedipus: Capitalism and Schizophrenia* that Bowie's focus on rude mechanicals could be seen as part of an intellectual zeitgeist manifesting itself at that moment and opposed to the dominant ideology of Human "spirit." In this groundbreaking book, Deleuze and Guattari advocate desire as a form of productive power in order to free it from the position in which psychoanalysis has tied it to notions of lack and absence. In order to do this, traditionally human, religious and anthropomorphic concepts such as "spirit", which presume a unity of being and purpose (and which constitutes the perfect patient for Freud and his descendents, paying for this elusive wholeness, transcendence, self-identity) are replaced by the notion of machines so that the body becomes "a desiring machine."[10] Every machine "is related to a continuous material flow (hyle: Greek for 'matter') that it cuts into and "each associative flow must be

---

[8] As heard on Bob Dylan Live, 1966. Royal Albert Hall Concert.
[9] Marshall McLuhan and Quentin Fiore, *The Medium is the Message,* 41.
[10] Gilles Deleuze and Félix Guattari, *Anti-Oedipus,* 9.

seen as an endless flux."[11] Language is one such flow and they believe that in the speech and actions of schizophrenics, deterritorialised desire finds its greatest expression. Given that Capitalism is itself a flow—"a flow of capital and a flow of labour as human surplus value [is] the industrial essence of capitalism"—and also a schizophrenic flow in its tendency to form "non-systematic associations of heterogeneous elements in its throwing together of workers and capital in any relation to make further money," [12] the intensification of schizophrenic language could possibly be a means of pushing capitalist logic to such extremes that it shatters. Through their argument, Deleuze and Guattari provide a path of resistance which arises from within the prevailing logic of capitalism, just as Marxism itself did before history began to suggest that Marxism somehow materialised in direct opposition to capitalism and therefore was unsullied by it.

Bowie's schizophrenic vision of mechanical human values allied with his tendency to describe characters on the edge and the constant spectre of his own schizophrenic brother haunting his writing style were all part of an innovative response to his cultural conditions that rebelled against the conventions of the late sixties singer-songwriter model. Bowie's debut thus proved that he was an artist with the foresight to engage (rather than simply condemn) the colonizing signs of capitalism and even attempt to distort them as an example of the type of resistant strategy that Deleuze and Guattari would later articulate within the French academy.

It is a feature of contemporary theory that the human subject and the concept of "Humanism" receive an enormous amount of scrutiny. In the following quotation, Patricia Waugh provides a succinct definition of the changing face of the human subject in the late twentieth century:

> For humanism, "man" is at the centre of meaning and action; the world is oriented around the individual. Each individual is different; each possesses a unique subjectivity; yet also, paradoxically, each shares a common human nature. The combination of unique individuality and common human essence coheres around the idea of a sovereign self, whose essential core of being transcends the outward signs of environmental and social conditioning. Post-structuralism has sought to disrupt this man-centred view of the world, arguing that the subject, and that sense of unique subjectivity itself, is constructed in language and discourse; and rather than being fixed and unified, the subject is split, unstable or fragmented.[13]

---

[11] Gilles Deleuze and Félix Guattari, *Ibid,* 17.
[12] Gilles Deleuze and Guattari, *Ibid,* 13.
[13] Patricia Waugh and Philip Rice, *Modern Literary Criticism,* 123.

Foreshadowing the fragmented subject, on *Hunky Dory* (1971) Bowie continued his deconstruction of "natural" or essential human values as the sovereign subject is assaulted from a number of directions. The lyrics and vocal delivery of "Ch-ch-ch-changes" is a model for a Derridean deconstruction of "the subject" based as they are on the absence of self-identical presence. Simply put, the stuttered delivery of the word "changes" stresses the word's lack of self-identity with itself, presenting real change as *différance*, different even to itself. "I turned myself to face me" suggests a multiplicity of selves replacing one centralised subject, and the use of the ripple metaphor—"I watch the ripples change their size" recalls the philosophic treatment of the river and the self by Heraclitus and Cratylus respectively, who came to the separate conclusions that you cannot put your foot in the same stream twice because both the river and the self change. [14]

His eponymous tribute to Andy Warhol— "Andy Warhol looks a scream / hang him on my wall / Andy Warhol / silver screen, can't tell them apart at all"—is a set of clever semantic gymnastics in which Bowie communicates his understanding of Warhol's desire to present himself and his personality as the art object. Through screen printing Warhol sells images from the screen (such as Marilyn Monroe) back to media hungry viewers as legitimate art. The flat screen (print), or surface, replaces more humanist notions of spiritual depth in art and foreshadows a society that will soon become dominated by the image. Similarly, in "Life on Mars" there is a reiteration of pleasure in the surface precisely because there is no depth in the worn-out world of images being sold to the audience as fresh entertainment. The narrator speaks of a girl who "is hooked to the silver screen / but the film is a saddening bore / for she's lived it ten times or more." The "girl with the mousy hair" responds to recycled plots and experiences with the sentiment that "she could spit in the eyes of fools / as they ask her to focus on/ sailors fighting in the dance hall" and asks, finally, "Is there life on Mars?" Well, within the year…

With *The Rise and Fall of Ziggy Stardust and the Spiders from Mars* (1972) Bowie continues his rebellion against Humanist idealism by continuing to challenge gender roles and notions of authenticity, going one step further here by inventing and playing the role of androgynous alien rock star. "The other," a philosophical term which has become synonymous with recent poststructuralist attempts to signify that which cannot easily be co-opted into Humanist binaries dependent on gender and ethnicity, seems almost designed to describe the Ziggy persona.[15] Further, in keeping with the constantly reappearing trope of surface,

---

[14] See T. V. Smith, *Philosophers Speak for Themselves: From Thales to Plato*, 13.

[15] For the most informed and exhaustive analysis of the applicability of Derrida's concept of "the other" see Geoffrey Bennington, *Jacques Derrida*. (Chicago: University of Chicago Press, 1999).

in the persona of Ziggy the politics of popular culture become a matter of style. As Dick Hebdige writes:

> Bowie as Ziggy was responsible for opening up questions of sexual identity which had previously been repressed, ignored or merely hinted at in rock and youth culture. In Bowie and Roxy Music the subversive emphasis was shifted away from class and youth onto sexuality and gender typing. [In this way they questioned] the value and meaning of adolescence and the transition to the adult world of work. And they did so in singular fashion, by artfully confounding the images of men and women through which the passage from childhood to maturity was traditionally accomplished.[16]

Of equal importance is that by presenting an artificial creation as the rock performer itself, Bowie stresses both the role of representation and the essentially contrived nature of pop performance, simultaneously. In short, he places irreversible emphasis on the disposable over the enduring and in so doing emphasizes the delicate yet incisive relevance of a popular culture trope that challenges depth with a symbolically invested "surface" politic.

In 1975, on *Young Americans*, Bowie flouted any notions of required style based on career curves, nationality or race. Indeed, for the next two years he would produce music and images that would register within the framework of cultural and national politics. Paul Gilroy writes that

> James Brown's "Say it loud I'm Black and I'm Proud," the ChiLites "Power to the People" and various versions of Weldon Irvine Jnr's "Young Gifted and Black" were all taken to the heart of black communities many miles from those in which they were created. These recordings are only the most obvious illustrations of the character of a period in which soul was revered as the principle criterion for affiliation to the black power movement.[17]

As the first white Soul boy (as opposed to Blues boys of which Lennon / McCartney and Jagger / Richards were among the first), Bowie attempted to critique the window of American life he had seen during the Ziggy Stardust tour by means of the primary cultural voice of its dispossessed black community: Soul music. The "Cracked Actor" film (1974), shot during the recording of *Young Americans*, follows a deferential but deeply enthusiastic white boy working with a multi-cultural band towards the idea of popular music as the site of cultural hybridity. As bell hooks asserts:

> If radical postmodernist thinking is to have a transformative impact, then a critical break with the notion of 'authority' as 'mastery over' must not simply be

---

[16] Dick Hebdige, *Subculture: the Meaning of Style,* 61-62.
[17] Paul Gilroy, *There Ain't no Black in the Union Jack,* 80.

a rhetorical device. It must be reflected in habits of being, including styles of writing as well as chosen subject matter. Third world nationals, elites and white critics who passively absorb white supremacist thinking, and therefore never notice or look at black people on the streets or at their jobs are not likely to produce liberatory theory that will challenge racist domination.[18]

By going to Philadelphia and immersing himself in the traditions of soul and the burgeoning culture of funk, Bowie reflects hooks's contention that

> It's exciting to think, write, talk about, and create art that reflects passionate engagement with popular culture, because this may well be "the" central future location of resistance struggle, a meeting place where new and radical happenings can occur.[19]

Consequently it can be argued that in a very productive way, *Young Americans* opened up soul music to white European audiences, and with it the possibility of wider cultural understanding. By bringing Soul to Paris and Peckham, Bowie played a large part in paving the way for inter-racial musical hybridity the influence of which can be seen today in as different an artist as Eminem.

By the mid-nineteen seventies Bowie had decamped to Berlin, a city torn by two competing economic and social philosophies. Disgruntled with his recording contract at RCA and under pressure to produce hits, he deliberately set out to create a low profile (verbally and visually represented on the artwork of *Low*) and two startlingly experimental albums, *Low* (1977) and *"Heroes"* (1997). Working without any clear pop sensibility or rock blueprint and producing more instrumental than vocal tracks, Bowie's Berlin period consolidated his reputation as the arch avant-garde musician of the pop/rock genre. While Punk rock was exploding across England and America, Bowie became a Kurtz like figure: distant, isolated, operating in the liminal spaces of his fan base's imagination. Of all of his experimental phases, his Berlin period remains resolutely "Other," unconsolidated in the genres of discourse that govern popular music reception.

However, *On Scary Monsters (and Super Creeps)* (1980), Bowie returned to the fray with surprisingly overt political lyrics, groundbreaking ideas for pop promo videos and renewed vigour for dynamic rock arrangements. Questions of third-world exploitation and Western isolationism hang in the air throughout the album:

> Silhouettes and shadows watch the revolution/no more three steps to Heaven / documentaries on refugees / couples 'gainst the target / they throw the rock against the road / and it breaks into pieces / put a bullet in my brain / and it

---

[18] bell hooks, "Postmodern Blackness", 419.
[19] bell hooks, *Ibid,* 423.

makes all the papers / so where's the moral when people have their fingers broken / to be insulted by these fascists—it's so degrading / and it's no game.

Schizophrenia tropes also recur on the song "Scary Monsters and Super Creeps" which documents a woman's nervous breakdown and "Scream Like a Baby" where the narrator "wouldn't buy the merchandise / and I wouldn't fight no war / And I mixed with other colours / But the nurse doesn't care" suggesting that between *Young Americans* and the isolation of the Berlin years Bowie recognised the rampant capitalism of Reaganism and Thatcherism slouching towards birth. Indeed, and perhaps as a positive—although doomed—primal scream against the aesthetic bankruptcy of the approaching decade, Bowie also has a seismic effect on the future of music video with the "Ashes to Ashes" (1980) promotional film. The video utilised a non-linear, non-sequential approach to the synergy of image and song. It organized its visualisation around metaphors rather than narrative logic in keeping with the brevity and non-linearity of the pop song. In other words, Bowie recognised that a three-minute film to accompany a song does not lend itself to narrative, but should be episodic and spatially orientated given that it is designed for multiple viewing rather than singular, or originary receipt. Thus in "Ashes to Ashes," which documents Major Tom's decline from astronaut to heroin addict (and so glosses the fallen idealism of the Sixties at the beginning of the Eighties), Bowie meanders under a black nuclear sky playing variously astronauts and asylum inmates. If one considers Baudrillard's suggestion (1983) that capital cannot be resisted morally or rationally but "is a challenge to take up according to symbolic law" (30) in conjunction with Deleuze and Guattari's call for the manifestation of schizophrenic impulses in art, then Bowie presents this impulse in the recurring asylum inmates and in the fragmentary nature of the video's form. Epic, narratised story board videos by Michael Jackson and Madonna that followed "Ashes to Ashes" as a promotional tool both rationalised the video format (turning it into a narrative story) and moralised it in Baudrillard's terms, emptying the format of its potential subversive capacity and so preparing it for many of the empty pastiches that we recognise as music video today. In contrast, the "Ashes to Ashes" video remains as the trace of the potential of a symbolically invested political art form.

In his article "Rock, Pop and Politics," John Street (2001) suggests that music is political in three ways: lyrically, formally and culturally, and towards two political positions: left and right. By remaining conservative at the lyrical, formal and cultural level, a large amount of popular music signifies exclusively on the right. In contrast, *Scary Monsters and Super Creeps* forges a critical synergy of the left; in Bowie's last great marginal album, lyrics, music and video signify richly in each of Street's three ways. Moreover, this synergy is executed as part of Bowie's well-established surfacing technique, stressing the very artificiality of the musical form he was attempting to render politically important. This, together with treatments of the recurrent tropes of schizophrenia, technology, and identity in his work, mark out 1969-1980s Bowie as one of the most aesthetically and politically important artists of the late twentieth century, and a key progenitor of postmodern discourse.

However, for the remainder of the eighties, Bowie made a very surprising move by alienating the audience he had developed during his career. Put simply, from *Let's Dance* (1983) onwards Bowie courted mainstream popularity. Certainly, the horrors of David Bowie dueting with Tina Turner in shameless attempts for chart credibility coupled with his instructions to Nile Rodgers "to produce hits,"[20] and his appearance with Mick Jagger in arguably the worst video of all time (and this despite its charitable intentions!) undermined his credibility with an audience that valued him for his experimentation and erstwhile subversive attitude towards mass popular culture. Finally, an attempt to regain some credibility with *Tin Machine* (1989) seemed to indicate that Bowie completely misread his early audience given that he was now trying to sell himself as authentic rocker returning to the basics of his chosen artistic form. By 1990 Bowie had been abandoned by that community referred to here as "early Bowie fans" because he was no longer an alternative to the mainstream; he was the mainstream in all of its banal mediocrity.

Reading Bowie Twice

David Bowie: This reminds me of a conversation I had with Keith Richards at the 1972 Weedon Convention. Keith said to me "What's the difference between a Lonnie Donegan B-side and a Derrida deconstruction?"

Brian Eno: There must be a great punch-line to this question. Perhaps this is what the journalist could supply? The first joke linking skiffle and post-structuralist philosophy.[21]

The preceding section of this essay is designed to convince the reader that Bowie's early work is ripe in experimentation and therefore rich in aesthetic politics; whether in the very discernible effect of his cultural influence (from Ziggy subcultures to inter-racial cross-cultural music affiliations) or in rewarding returns from more theoretical forms of consideration. However, a certain operation has also taken place in the preceding section. Any subversive significance attributable to Bowie has been generated by aligning his work with a certain post-Marxist strain of thought (Derrida, Deleuze, etc.). This can be

---

[20] David Buckley, *Strange Fascination,* 391.
[21]"Conversation between Bowie and Eno", *Q* Magazine, 26/10/1994.

considered a strategy in which my subjective preference for early Bowie has been rendered academically legitimate due to a complementarity between celebrated theory and Bowie's artistic practice.

Yet the crux of the matter is that it is just as easy for contemporary Bowie fans to construct a convincing argument about Bowie's continued importance based on his popularity, accessibility and Internet availability. As documented earlier, this latter position is made possible by the alteration in the manner in which popular culture investigation appraises its subject. From the initial nineteen-eighties observations undertaken by Hebdige and Frith regarding how subcultural movements enact a positive resistance to homogenisation, popular culture studies has moved into the new millennium mainstream without discriminating in its choice of music or artists, but determined to inscribe and empower. What is most interesting is that the shift in Bowie's career from the margins to the mainstream is coterminous with the change in the popular culture theory paradigm: Bowie and theory went from valuing the alternative to embracing the majority. The result is that by default the new approach renders problematic any determination of Bowie's earlier marginality as politically valuable. Under the terms of the second discourse, it is only by *being* mainstream and accessible that the artist is politically useful. Effectively, the second discourse cancels out the value of the first one. Worse, at its point of lowest common denomination the second theoretical discourse implies that early Bowie fans were simply enacting bourgeois stratification through their choice of music, which in the idiom of rock and roll seems patently absurd. Nonetheless, according to the modus operandi of the second, more recent popular culture discourse, the original discourse is a dangerous thing because it facilitates audiences who believe they are enacting subversive musical preference as a symbolic political act, but who are in fact attempting to enforce economic stratification through the notion of refined taste. In the final analysis, the populist popular discourse distorts the nature of the fan in grotesque ways which is all the more absurd given that its rationale was to properly represent the popular culture consumer. By default, in legitimating populist fans it denigrates those fans that perceived a rebellious social value in rock and roll, and further reduces any chance of this discourse growing exponentially.

The objective of this essay was to show how meaning is inscribed by the nature of discourse; to reiterate Barthes' principle (1972) that "myth is a type of speech."[22] Both of the discourses outlined here are examples of imposed value—one no more than the other—but in Bowie's case it would appear that one can only be imposed at the expense of the other. As a result of a shift in the nature of the interpretative discourse at a time when Bowie's popularity also shifted, to prioritise Bowie's early career on the grounds of its rebelliousness

---

[22] Roland Barthes, "Myth Today", 117.

and resistance to capital is to consign it to false consciousness and limited use value. The final paradox is this: if we consider that a critic recognises the manner in which artists can be read according to the agendas of certain discourses, how then can one be expected to read Bowie's entire career to date? If it must be read irrespective of its resistance to capital—which requires a specialised discourse to tease out its lyrical, cultural and formal innovations—then much of his early work fails to signify. Further, if Bowie is now an important source of popular culture study as a result of how his accessible audio-visual Internet activity can be read, then his earlier stylistic "subversions" are an irrelevant component in the ways in which rock music can affect political change. He simply had to be accessible and popular rather than elusive and aloof in the first place. Early Bowie fans may even reflect that in the manner in which access to information and the concomitant demystification of ideology can empower people, Bowie's late-seventies ambient sound-scapes come a poor second … in the wrong discourse!

Finally, in no other artist in rock are the principle differences between modes of critical representation so obvious. Essentially, the discourse of postmodernism would not be so easily consolidated within the humanities, and hardly at all within the rock idiom, without one of its key cast members, and certainly Bowie's work would not assume primacy in any analysis of influence and effect in rock music were it not for his "revolutionary" effect in the nineteen-seventies. And yet, it is precisely these qualities that must now be silenced in order to validate a voice for an alternative discourse that seeks to find empowerment in other artists, and, paradoxically, in Bowie himself. The result is that narrative treatments of the legacy of David Bowie will always say less about Bowie and his work, and more about the discourses and relationships between the discourses that are used to represent him. The strength of this legacy is that it will unfailingly interrogate the evolution of popular culture studies as an academic discourse.

References

Adorno, Theodor W. "On Popular Music" (1941). Reprinted in *The Culture Industry: Selected Essays on Mass Culture*, edited by J. M. Bernstein, 70-93. London: Routledge, 1991.

Barthes, Roland. "Myth Today." In *Image-Music-Text*, 14-34. Trans. Stephen Heath. London: Collins, 1972.

Baudrillard, Jean. *Simulations*. NewYork: Semiotext(e), 1983.

Bennington, Geoffrey. *Jacques Derrida*. Chicago: University of Chicago Press, 1999.

Buckley, David. *Strange Fascination: David Bowie, the Definitive Story*. Virgin Books: London, 1999.

Butler, Judith. *Gender Trouble*. London: Routledge, 1999.

Deleuze, Gilles and Félix Guattari. *Anti-Oedipus: Capitalism and Schizophrenia*. Trans. Robert Hurley, Mark Seem and Helen R. Lane. London: The Athlone Press, 1984.

Du Noyer, Paul. "ChangesFiftyBowie" *Q* Magazine April, 1997. Available at http://www.bowiewonderworld.com/press/press90.htm

Fiske, John. "Cultural Studies and the Culture of Everyday Life." In *Cultural Studies*, edited by Lawrence Grossberg, Cary Nelson and Paula Treicher, 154-174. London: Routledge, 1992.

Frith, Simon. "The Good, the Bad, and the Indifferent: Defending Popular Culture from the Populists." *Cultural Theory and Popular Culture: A Reader*, edited by John Storey, 570-586. Hertfordshire: Prentice Hall, 1998.

Gilroy, Paul. *There Ain't no Black in the Union Jack*. London: Hutchinson, 1987.

Hebdige, Dick. *Subculture: The Meaning of Style*. New York: Routledge, 1979.

hooks, bell. "Postmodern Blackness"(1991). In *Cultural Theory and Popular Culture: A Reader,* edited by John Storey , 417-425. Hertfordshire: Prentice Hall, 1998.

McLuhan, Marshall & Quentin Fiore. *The Medium is the Massage*. New York: Bantam Books, 1967.

Paglia, Camille. *Vamps and Tramps*. London: Vintage, 1994.

Q Magazine. "Conversation between Bowie and Eno" 26/10/94. Available at http://www.bowiewonderworld.com/press/press90.htm

Shakespeare, William. *Hamlet*. London: Routledge, 1993.

Smith, T. V. *Philosophers Speak for Themselves: From Thales to Plato*. Chicago and Phoenix: University of Chicago Press, 1956.

Street, John. "Rock, Pop and Politics." In *The Cambridge Companion to Pop and Rock*, edited by Simon Frith, Will Straw and John Street, 243-256. Cambridge: Cambridge University Press, 2001.

Sutherland, Steve. "Bowie: Boys Keep Swinging." *Melody Maker* 24 No. 4 (1990): 23-29. Available at:
http://www.bowiewonderworld.com/press/press90.htm

Waugh, Patricia and Philip Rice. *Modern Literary Theory*. London: Arnold, 1989.

Willis, David. *The Social Dimension of Popular Music*. Birmingham: University of Birmingham Press, 1974.

Yentob, Alan. *Cracked Actor*, BBC Productions, 1974.

Discography

Bowie, David, *Space Oddity*. Philips, 1969.

———. *Hunky Dory*. RCA, 1971.

———. *The Rise and Fall of Ziggy Stardust and the Spiders from Mars*. RCA, 1972.

———. *Young Americans*. RCA, 1975.

———. *Low*. RCA, 1977.

———. *"Heroes."* RCA, 1977.

———. *Scary Monsters (and Super Creeps)*. RCA, 1980.

———. *Let's Dance*. EMI, 1983.

———. *Tin Machine*. EMI, 1989.

———. *Heathen*. ISO/Sony. 2002.

Dylan, Bob. *Bob Dylan Live, 1966. Royal Albert Hall Concert, Bootleg Series, Vol. 4*. Columbia, 1996.

CHAPTER FOUR

PRISMATICS OF MUSIC AND CULTURE: THE EQUIVOCATION OF NORDIC METAL

İBRAHIM BEYAZOĞLU

Abstract: This paper explores the explosion of obnoxious Nordic Metal onto the scene in the 1990s. İbrahim Beyazoğlu is experientially familiar with the ethos of Nordic Metal, even if he has since buried the paraphernalia deep under the innocence of his back garden. There is thus an issue of identity for this writer. What better mechanism then for the articulation of the nexus of identity, popular musical practice and concept formation than that old draught-horse of self-apprehending ontological structures, the Hegelian dialectic, without, of course, direct mention of Georg Wilhelm Friedrich himself. What saves the dialectic, in this paper, from the fate of Narcissus, is the welcome plunge into ambiguity on the way to ontological purity: The master becomes the slave and the slave the master. Popular music may be liberating in a Fiskean way, or oppressive, in the way diagnosed by Adorno's blackmail effect. Beyazoğlu, without rejecting the political import of cultural activity and cultural studies, rehearses the familiar arguments, looking for ways out of the little thought traps that we fall into, often while hugging a warm beer and nodding sagely at the back of a concert hall or holding forth in the lecture halls of academia. The conclusion is that nothing can be done, in Beckettian fashion. One must simply keep talking, posing questions and reaching deeper into the invigorating murk of ambiguity. That much is certain. But in talking there is a dynamic, without which criticism faces a kind of "intellectual death-by-chocolate": The imaginative engagement of the critic!

> Waves that leap like waves must fall.[1]
> Nothing can slake my thirst for the nameless and the obscure.[2]

This paper offers a descriptive and critical analysis of the way in which elements of Old Norse mythology are used in the musical products of contemporary Scandinavian Metal bands. Of particular interest are the cultural and ideological

---

[1]Mihai Eminescu, *Gloss*. Retrieved December 5th, 2005 from:
http://www.mihaieminescu.ro/en/literary_work/poems/gloss.htm
[2] Charles Baudelaire, "Sympathetic Horror", 122.

transformations that occur in this mythological material within the context of the market economy of the culture industry. The theoretical problematic around which this paper is oriented derives from the double aspect of Nordic Metal interpretations: On the one hand, selected elements of Old Norse mythology are used for the purposes of ethnicist mythmaking, thus bolstering nationalist ideologies of Nordic Metal bands which present themselves as the radical opponents of the prevalent system. On the other hand, the political and ideological positions represented in the music and lyrics of Nordic Metal bands undergo a process of attenuation when they gain ground in the contemporary culture industry.

In general, research on the influence of Norse mythology on the products falling into the frame of the culture industry is scarce. There are two reasons for this: Firstly, Norse mythology has been tainted by its association with fascism in Northern Europe during the middle part of twentieth century. Currently, this issue has taken the form of a conflict between the "academic construction of the past" and "other constructions of the past considered meaningful for some groups in society".[3] Consequently, students of Nordic paganism are concerned that their scholarly activity may contribute to the "destructive" use of Nordic mythology found in emergent racist trends in Scandinavian societies. Secondly, as Mike Jones has argued, "popular music is the least considered area of Media and Cultural Studies", mainly because of its "pop" nature.[4] According to Jones, the term "pop" is generally used with a sense of disdain and popular music products are considered too shallow and fleeting to be the subject of serious academic study. The case of Nordic Metal is even more complicated, because until the late 1990s, Viking Metal groups and Scandinavian bands incorporating themes of Old Norse mythology remained "underground", too marginal to be considered part of popular music.

In the 1990s, Old Norse mythology underwent yet another revival, this time at the hands of Nordic Metal bands. This movement falls under two categories: Viking Metal, which gravitated towards the pagan beliefs of Norse mythology and the historical Viking period, took a populist antichristian, antisystem direction. In general, there was no active violent challenge to society in this branch of the movement. On the other hand, Black Metal developed a destructive and hostile stance to the *status quo*, cultivating a satanic neoPagan-Nazi posture. Historically speaking, Punk, Rock, Hard Rock, and Heavy Metal made headway through their strong critical stance and always bore a destructive potential. However, the Nordic Metal bands, Black Metal in particular, were the first ever to turn their musical ancestors' destructive possibility into discredited reality. In the early 1990s bands like Burzum, Darkthrone, Emperor and

---

[3] Atle Omland, "Catharine Raudvere, Anders Andrén and Kristina Jennbert", 86.
[4] Mike Jones, "The Music Industry as Workplace", 147.

Mayhem concentrated the drive to replace Christianity and other received social norms with Old Norse mythology, and norms and customs from the Viking period. In this atmosphere, churches were set on fire, and, within this circle of activity, several highly publicized murders took place. It was these crime-embedded acts in the context of the genre that pioneered and introduced Nordic Metal to the world.

In the late 1990s the ethos and music of these bands underwent a kind of "taming process", mainly as a result of submission to social hegemonic factors and the real legal and financial pressures of the culture industry. What society had failed to do, namely the silencing of these bands through what is perceived as "commonsense", was achieved by the power of Capital. There were of course interventions by the more "muscular" forces of the state apparatus. Some leading members were given prison sentences or said to have been taken into custody for questioning. However, from a Gramscian perspective, hegemony works not by forcefully imposing its will, but by producing will by the means of "commonsense" phenomena so as to legitimize prevailing norms.[5] Hence Gramsci's centaur allegory: In some cases, subversive acts necessitated Black Metal to be treated as the bestial part of the centaur, while the Viking Metal credo was dealt with as the human part of the centaur.

Modern, capitalist societies have invented a paradoxical mechanism for the effective "defanging" of social movements that seek to subvert the *status quo*. The exercise of freedom of expression may of course effectively inhibit hegemonic structures in society. The same thing, however, may also produce the opposite effect, with freedom of expression effectively taking the edge off otherwise subversive discourse. The chasing down of radical social movements to their underground organizational roots under certain circumstances results in a form of collaboration, especially if violent means are used. By contrast, it is the manner of the capitalist system to usher the radical perspective from its subterranean milieu out into the open of the market place, in the process dulling the trajectory, density and rigidity of hard-hitting ideologies so that they appear packaged, "manicured" and commodified.[6] Thus a strategy, which may be expressed as a kind of "daylight robbery", is implemented to preserve mainstream social and economic interests. Resistance and extremism are used against themselves in the capitalist system. In the case under discussion, Nordic Metal turned into its own antidote in evasion of its own self-mythologized project of social resistance. Accordingly, Roland Barthes maintains that

> It thus appears ... extremely difficult to vanquish myth from the inside: for the very effort one makes in order to escape its strangle hold becomes in its turn the

---

[5] Carl Boggs, "What Gramsci Means Today", 66.
[6] Michael Moynihan and Didrik Søderlind, *Lords of Chaos*, xvi.

prey of myth: myth can always, as a last resort, signify the resistance which is brought to bear against it. Truth to tell, the best weapon against myth is perhaps to mythify it in its turn, and to produce an *artificial myth*: and this reconstituted myth will in fact be a mythology.[7]

When the Nordic Metal ethos was transformed into a relatively innocent amusement popularized and commercialised for the Metal scene, it forwent its sharp ideological point of view and the system continued in safety compared to early 1990s. According to Dick Hebdige, the pressure of the press is highly effective in the incorporation process. More concisely, the media operates in line with both hegemonic sides. It simultaneously detects and markets subterranean acts by provoking, in Hebdige's words, a "hysteria" that "is typically ambivalent: It fluctuates between dread and fascination, outrage and amusement."[8] The media operates as a guardian of those interests that tend to be dominant in society. As suggested by the Shoemaker research, the media do not screen out deviant ideas but rather portray them in a way calculated to underscore their deviance. The ideological *status quo* is reaffirmed by ridiculing "deviant" ideas.[9]

As Nordic Metal bands got involved in the culture industry, their musical output developed towards a more popular direction, and artists had the chance to perform in better conditions. The mentality and opinions of some of the fans, bands and artists gradually changed from an initial simplistic, wayward and dogmatic prototype to a somewhat pragmatic, worldly, materialistic, realistic type. The culture industry and legal system both work by imposing inconspicuous force and consent-producing practices through, for example, the discipline imposed by a contract with a record company. As a result, labels do not impose force upon the artist in signing the contract, but after the parties enter into an agreement, there arises a more subtle threat. Contractual liabilities and stipulations are compulsory, authoritative and deterrent: "When a pop act signs a record contract it signs just that, a contract to record—not one to release, promote, market or distribute records. Pop acts are powerless to initiate and prosecute these decisive activities."[10] In some cases, discouraging consequences await the artist in case of violations of the contract. Infringement may shorten the duration of a band in a particular genre. Learning how to reap financial reward to sidestep trouble is integral to a band's continued existence in any genre. Bands finding themselves at a disadvantage are impelled into releasing quick albums to make sure that they fulfill contract obligations.

---

[7] Roland Barthes, *Mythologies*, 135.
[8] Dick Hebdige, *Subculture: The Meaning of Style*, 92.
[9] P. J. Shoemaker and S. D. Reese, *Mediating the Message*, 225.
[10] Mike Jones, "The Music Industry as Workplace", 153.

To use an indigenous Scandinavian metaphor, there is something troll-like in the fate of Nordic metal in the market economy. Just as the troll is petrified when exposed to the light of day, losing its substantial power on venturing from the darkness of its cave, so the Nordic metal band suffers the loss of its thunder in the so-called openness of the market place.[11] After those bands entered the mainstream milieu, the unpopular and alternative stance against the social and political system gradually lessens or totally vanishes. After a short while, they rupture and end up like a troll. Such popularity, as is gained in the market place, is a pseudo-freedom of expression aimed at taking the trolls out of their unreachable dark places where they thrive.

The pronouncements of Nordic Metal, as well as the typical contents of Metal lyrics, operate on the basis of a unitarist, exclusionist language. The question of identity in such language is fixed to the imagined ethos of a past age and an imagined "other", which must at all cost be marked out and excluded from the centre where signification is produced and maintained. The Nordic Metal centre emphasizes the "invariable presences" of "the North," "true Metal," "Paganism," "the Vikings," "Satan," and "the Underground." As ground for an orthodox, centered way of thinking, the Nordic Metal league views its constitution in a positive light. The transcendentalising of key terms, placing them above the fluctuations that happen at the level of everyday use of language, confine meaning to an imagined whole. Anybody who wants to follow the Nordic Metal movement is obliged to see the world through the eyes of a controlling prototype. Given the internal formation of the Viking or Black Metal ethos in terms of epistemological and physical violence, dialogue within this context is a profoundly sedimentary, Procrustean phenomenon.

There is a kind of sovereignty at play in Nordic metal discourse, one which is propped up by a core set of binary oppositions, such as harsh music / listenable music, Scandinavian / nonScandinavian, Northern / Southern, true metal / false metal, dirty sound / clean sound, Pagan / Christian, underground / mainstream, virility / effeminacy, male / female, and so on. Through such simplistic binary oppositions, communication processes are at once strictly circumscribed and deeply internalized by the bands and the audience in agreed texts. Once codified, the bond between the signifier and signified becomes highly inflexible and anchors discourse in a set of narrow, prejudicial and ultimately self-serving slogans that are put beyond criticism. So, for example, to release a CD with one of the bigger Metal labels is said to be a kind of hypocrisy, even "gayness". Music produced on a low budget using the loved "dirty sound" is seen as "true music." In a disturbing regression to the vicious scapegoatism of the fascist past, "homosexuality", "communism" and "Jewishness" are conflated and denounced. To appeal to wide audiences is to

---

[11] I owe this analogy to my friend, Bitte Kristin Emberland.

"sell out", which is considered a great act of betrayal. Selling limited "dirty-sounding," "underground" music is to be faithful to the cause of Nordic Metal, "Northernness" and even, "Norway".

Nordic Metal's hermeneutics of the recording industry clings to a paradigm constituted by such binary oppositions as "faithful / sellout", "insider / outsider", "authentic / inauthentic", "labour of love / money grubbing". In the early 1990s, in an attempt to satisfy the culture industry, the popular cutting-edge tendency of Nordic Metal identified itself with "underground" values and projected the prevailing system and music recording industry in general as if it were divided into the imaginary boundaries mentioned above. In order to be free from the all-encompassing reach of the capitalist monolith, Nordic Metal incorporated into its esoteric ideology an aesthetics of "true" Metal. Music would conform to a certain predetermined standard, and records would be hard to acquire. Above all, the musical aesthetics of Nordic Metal would be straightforward and musically unappealing. Otherwise, it would be indistinguishable from the stigmatized popular, higher selling metal, which in Nordic Metal's vocabulary was considered "Gay Music" or "Pink Metal", thus appropriating for their own music a highly dubious "masculinity". A tight knit scene developed in Norway under the slogan "No fun, no mosh, no trends, no core",[12] and pioneers of the genre dogmatically admonished their loyal devotees to stay outside the social system with a select group of dedicated individuals. Mayhem's Aarseth pours scorn on the popular genre: "We should meet up at concerts and beat up ALL trend people ALL the time until they would be too scared to go to concert at all."[13] The following quotation from Aarseth gives a description of the accident-prone, cultic and underground propensities of Black Metal:

> I don't think people should respect each other. I don't want to see trend people respecting me, I want to them to HATE and to FEAR. If people don't accept our ideas as their own, they can fuck off because then they belong to a musical scene which has NOTHING to do with ours. They could just as well be Madonna fans. There is an ABYSS between us and the rest. Remember, one of the Hardcore Punk rules is that [everyone] must be open-minded, except for themselves, so we must be careful and avoid being open-minded ourselves.[14]

Poststructuralism has endowed us with the principal that linguistic signification is nothing but the ever flowing and falling of dominos. It must be asked whether the project of insisting on a static relation between the signifier and signified is at all viable. According to Jacques Derrida,

---

[12] Keith Kahn-Harris, "The Failure of Youth Culture," 99.
[13] Michael Moynihan and Didrik Søderlind, *Lords of Chaos*, 79.
[14] Michael Moynihan and Didrik Søderlind, *Ibid*, 79.

> the center also closes off play which it opens up and makes possible. As center, it is the point at which the substitution of contents, elements, or terms is no longer possible. At the center, the permutation or the transformation of elements is forbidden ... The center is the center of the totality.[15]

Thus the tendency towards closure in Nordic Metal discourse is, more than anything else, an internal discipline aimed at neutralising the differential dynamics of language and symbolic systems of meaning. Within this totality of meaning, time and space are frozen in a single frame, a frame through which all subsequent meaning production will be directed. It is an ideology of certainty generated and presided over by the physical and epistemological violence of the movements that made up Nordic Metal. However, the signifier is not necessarily connected to the signified as it appears in Nordic Metal beliefs and productions. Cultural war on the differential and elusive nature of meaning always meets with confrontations, refractions and counter-struggles.

It is the argument of this paper that Nordic Metal's strategic separation of itself from the culture industry through the deployment of imagined, metaphysical boundaries is neither an act of effective resistance, nor a radical "antisystem" act. Nor is it a movement of liberation, but rather, if we adopt Theodore Adorno's perspective, a manifestation of capital in its negative model: "The dreams have no dream ... There is nothing more practical than escape, nothing more fervently espoused to big business."[16] The economic and cultural system is already omnipotent, invisible and immanent in the individual through the process of language learning and acculturation. It is like a space where, paradoxically, every single point is the centre. The social and economic system supplies the items to make music with. Books, fanzines, magazines are provided by the market economy. Musical instruments come from the cultural and economic system. Most significantly, it is again the system which made available the CDs VCDs, DVDs to record music: "Media culture provides materials to create identities whereby individuals insert themselves into contemporary techno-capitalist societies and which is producing a new form of the global culture."[17] All destructive ideas appear by means of the market economy so that as people fall under their influence, the market is extended and accordingly developed; consequently capital will be saved. Therefore, Nordic Metal's tendency to see itself at the margins of the cultural system can not be regarded as tenable. Dick Hebdige claims that subcultures are not alternative to, or separate from the production of the system:

---

[15] Jacques Derrida, *Writing and Difference*, 279.

[16] Theodor Adorno, *Minima Moralia*, 202.

[17] Douglas Kellner, *Media Culture*, 1.

Clearly, subcultures are not privileged forms; they do not stand outside the
reflexive circuitry of production and reproduction which links together, at least
on a symbolic level, the separate and fragmented pieces of the social totality.[18]

The system is an intense and penetrative process, which tends not to fragment,
but to remain intact despite there being confrontation in it. As Michel Foucault
observes, "resistance is never in a position of exteriority in relation to power."[19]
Nordic or Viking Metal can neither symbolically nor physically keep on acting
as if the artist were outside of the system, as the culture industry is adept at
absorbing oppositional and dissenting voices into the mainstream as commercial
products, thus creating a kind of theatrical spectacle.

Moreover, it is pointless to be lured into a "strange occultation"[20] to destroy a
system that in turn feeds and maintains itself by means of its own self-
destruction.[21] It adapts itself to changes and crises or develops parallel to the
developments as the system keeps track of all motion. Late capitalism is
metabolic; it eats, digests and has its moment of *jouissance* and then perseveres
in line with the turmoil. Promethean, subterranean utopias with their creativity
and upheaval are also, at the same time, not unlike the never-ending handiwork
of Penelope's loom. As Guiseppe Di Lampadusa remarks in his treatise on
change, the ironically titled *The Leopard,* "if we want things to stay as they are,
things will have to change."[22] The culture industry always works steadily and
recycles in set periods. Audiences do not demand new meaning from the
products of the culture industry: "The bastard form of mass culture is humiliated
repetition."[23] Although Barthes identifies succinctly the cyclic nature of cultural
production and reproduction, it is possible to discern in the language he uses a
bias against popular culture and the hidden assumption that an alternative
cultural form belies less of the "bastard element", a cultural form, let us say, that
is self-consciously aware of its contradictions. Hence the Romantic division of
the world into high culture and mass culture, the one thoughtful and
emancipatory, the other crude, spectacular and demeaning. There is another point
of view, which would deconstruct the dichotomy of high culture and mass
culture, offering instead the argument that all cultural expression may in equal
measure be liberating or oppressive. Now we are in a binary trap, one
disturbingly similar to Nordic Metal's "insider / outsider" and "faithful / sellout." After all, all blackmail is the same. At this point, this essay treads

---

[18] Dick Hebdige, *Subculture: the Meaning of Style*, 85-86.

[19] Michel Foucault, *The History of Sexuality*, 95.

[20] Frederic Jameson, *Postmodernism,* 20.

[21] Marshall Berman, *All that is Solid Melts into Air,* 57.

[22] Guiseppe Tomassi Di Lampedusa, *The Leopard*, 22.

[23] Roland Barthes, *The Pleasure of the Text,* 41.

nervously into this politico-ethical swamp. The certainties of Nordic Metal cut both ways.

With writers like Theodor Adorno, Max Horkheimer and Herbert Marcuse the culture industry is seen as something that feeds off the weak, helpless and naïve consumer. Marcuse argues that the culture industry has successfully flattened modern societies into a one-dimensional plane, thus creating pliancy, docility and an enthusiasm for the fleeting.[24] In the same way, for Adorno and Horkheimer, the system is not liberating but tyrannical: "The culture industry does not sublimate; it represses".[25] This model takes for granted that the audience's thinking patterns have been previously determined, and that the individual is inevitably passive, to the extent of being almost nothing, slightly absent, despite a seeming presence—expressed in the phrase, "beings without spirit."[26] From this perspective the culture industry is concerned with profit only, and to this end it provides entertainment; a process of penetration whose sole aim is the binding of audience to producer. The semantic mechanism that organizes, articulates and sustains this process of penetration, as it appears in Adorno, is that of the binary opposition: intelligence / stupidity, good / evil, salvation / captivity, originality / banality, reason / myth, rational / irrational, seriousness / entertainment."[27] Adorno detested popular music for its simplistic structure, which, he insisted, was designed to predispose the audience to mass-consumption. According to his view, the audience of pop music takes on the characteristics of the commodity it encounters in the market place, passive yet omnivorous in its reception patterns. Adorno asserts that there is a neurotic mechanism of stupidity in listening; the arrogantly ignorant rejection of everything unfamiliar is its sure sign. Regressive listeners behave like children.[28]

The alternative to Adorno's important and trenchant critical stance emerges from Antonio Gramsci's notion of hegemony and counter-hegemony, wherein cultural practices and the means of production, within which they are inevitably framed in late capitalist society are in fact locked into a "moving equilibrium."[29] Here the binary oppositions, let us say, of the kind we see in Adorno and, technically, Nordic metal, are not mutually exclusive, but are locked into a resistance struggle of hegemony / counter-hegemony, and thus meaning is produced in a dialectic of ever-shifting categories. For the most part John Fiske and those who align themselves, more or less loosely, with this strategy are inclined to regard the link that binds cultural manufacturer, producer and

---

[24] Herbert Marcuse, *One Dimensional Man*, 11.

[25] Theodor Adorno and Max Horkheimer, *Dialectic of Enlightenment*, 140.

[26] Marshall Berman, *All that is Solid Melts into Air,* 26.

[27] Knut Lundby and Helge Ronning, "Media-Culture-Communication," 266.

[28] Keith Negus, "Popular Music: between Celebration and Despair," 383.

[29] Dick Hebdige, *Subculture: the Meaning of Style,* 16.

audience as a negotiated agency, wherein cultural engagement is an act of interpretation that encodes the text in question, whether it be Nordic Metal, Beethoven, Dostoyevsky or Walt Disney.[30] Resistance may be characterized semiotically in its propensity to create new meanings, displacing dominant texts and evading the stereotypes preferred by the culture industry. For Fiske, the system no longer oppresses from top to bottom but, vice versa, from a semiotic perspective, meaning and power are being produced too from the grassroots up. The cultural system is an immense, powerful but clumsy giant, typically replete with weakness and vulnerability, indicating real possibilities for cultural resistance. The wider the scope of its influence, the more space opens up for subversion. In particular, and this flies in the face of Adorno's asceticism, resistance is not incompatible with pleasure: "popular pleasures as opposed to hegemonic ones".[31]

With these thoughts in mind, the critical stance against Nordic Metal's fascistic closing down of the meaning-producing mechanism of free-play becomes problematic. In Viking Metal, the pleasure moments are self evident at concerts, in visual images of fans and the spectacular deeds of band members. *Jouissance* is losing the self through blissful hedonistic pleasure. So musically, Viking Metal may be construed as a sort of evasion of the prevailing power. For example, many Nordic Metal concerts overlay catchy melody and rhythm with intense, high-decibel noise and stirring and aggressive antics from band members on the stage. The fans relentlessly bounce, scream, push each other, jump, dance with joy and rage, headbang like ones possessed and practice stage-diving. The cultural studies critic thus finds him or herself in a bind of ambivalence; fascist tendencies, inciting hatred, self-proclaimed outsiders on the one hand; on the other hand, pathetic, deluded demagogues lining their own pockets through the agency of impossible self-mythologization. On the other hand again (let's evade the logic of the binary opposition), the musical experience of Nordic Metal is deeply compelling in its wildly enthusiastic and cathartic pleasure, and thereby, according to the Fiskean thesis, subversive within the context of the culture industry.

If these two models were not postulated, cultural theorists would not go any further. Cultural studies itself is part of the culture industry. Theorists do not sit outside cultural practice providing solutions as if from above. Neither am I pointing to dialectics. Theorists enter a discourse, which in turn throws out its tendrils. In this sense, theoretical discourse is simply part of the entire mélange, the imaginative refraction of Eros and Thanatos, two forces locked in paradox. It is here considered superfluous to label Adorno a cultural fascist in the elite mode, nor Fiske a head-banger. Academic discourse on the culture industry feeds

---

[30] John Fiske, *Understanding Popular Culture*, 40-43.
[31] John Fiske, *Ibid*, 49.

off cultural practice, in what Pierre Bourdieu terms the "academic market."[32] As Bourdieu remarks, academics produce

> another market, with its own consecrating agencies, that is, like the high-society or intellectual markets, capable of challenging the pretension of the educational system to impose the principles of evaluation of competences and manners which reign in the scholastic market, or at least its most scholastic sectors, on a perfectly united market in cultural goods.[33]

Following this line of thought, it may be noted that academic works such as Fiske's popular culture studies and Hebdige's work on subcultures, treatises on The Doors and David Bowie have occasioned immense curiosity both in the musical scenes themselves and the academic environment. Music and cultural comment to a large extent appear to be serving both capital and hyping and appreciating subcultural scenes. Invoking attention via such critical and analytic works, scholars and the subcultural actors are urged to read more texts to perpetuate the system. As Simon Frith comments,

> the paradox is that in making pop music a site for the play of their fantasies and anxieties, intellectuals (and I think this process has a rather long history rather than that of cultural studies) have enriched this site for everyone else too.[34]

The aim of this essay was not the stabilization of the music and culture debate. Nor did it attempt to set forth some novel and important solution to the theoretical impasses that characterize cultural studies. As a matter of fact this paper contributes nothing. In the discipline, arguments accumulate around polarized formations in an attempt to reconcile the fierce Manichean-like predicament of the cultural studies debate. While once the field looked into music and culture, now it is preoccupied with tracking down the original reasons for this dispute. Concerning the foregoing impasse, debate is polarized using the same techniques Nordic Metal uses to stifle the imagination of its followers; namely, mystification. The anachronistic juxtaposing of the positions of Adorno and Fiske works to obscure crucial ambiguity and harden it into a monologic discourse. However, as Mikhail Bakhtin has said, the world's last word with regard to the world has not been said yet. Everything is still on the horizon and it always will be.[35] Since nothing alone can be good or bad, the core of the matter is the necessity to understand how the people surmount contradictions one by one rather than discovering what is right and what is wrong. As Barthes argues, the critic should "try to describe the acceptability of works, not their meaning.

---

[32] Pierre Bourdieu, *Distinction*, 13.
[33] Pierre Bourdieu, *Ibid*, 96.
[34] Simon Frith, "The Cultural Study of Popular Music," 179.
[35] Mikhail Bakhtin, *Problems of Dostoyevsky's Poetics*, 166.

We shall not classify the whole set of meanings as belonging to immutable order of things."[36]

Accordingly, I would like discuss the idea that posing problems is as valuable as giving answers to them. This paper would simply demand the right to pose new questions. Insisting on questioning in favour of remedial conclusions will at least lay profound stress on theoretical methodologies. Many traces are left behind and as these traces are removed, new traces are also left behind. In successfully solving a pressing problem, Oedipus brought about his own death. Therefore, we are responsible far beyond our intentions. Knowledge, on account of its form, is changeable and vulnerable to paradigmatic shifts. The problem as Heidegger claimed is itself is a way or method. Could this mean that ambiguity is the posing of the question itself as a way?

References

Adorno, Theodor. W. and Max Horkheimer. *Dialectic of Enlightenment*. Trans. J. Cumming. London: Verso, 1995.

————. *Minima Moralia*. Trans. E.F.N. Jephcott. London: Verso, 1996.

Bakhtin, Mikhail. *Problems of Dostoevsky's Poetics*. Trans. Caryl Emerson. Minneapolis: University of Minnesota Press, 2003.

Barthes, Roland. *Criticism and Truth*. Trans. K. P. Keuneman. London: The Athlone Press, 1998.

————. *The Pleasure of the Text*. New York: Hill and Wang, 1996.

————. *Mythologies*. Trans. A. Lavers. London: Vintage Books, 1993.

Baudelaire, Charles. "Sympathetic Horror." In *Poems*, trans. R. Howard and M. Hamburger. London: Everyman, 1993.

Berman, Marshall. *All that is Solid Melts into Air*. London & New York: Verso, 1983.

Boggs, Carl. "What Gramsci Means Today." In *Understanding Capitalism*, edited by Douglas Dowd, 57-81. London: Pluto Press, 2002.

Bourdieu, Pierre. *Distinction*. Trans. R. Nice. London: Routledge, 2003.

Derrida, Jacques. *Writing and Difference*. Trans. A. Bass. Chicago: The University of Chicago Press, 1978.

Di Lampedusa, Guiseppe Tomassi. *The Leopard*. Trans. A. Colquhoun. London: Everyman's Library, 1998.

Eminescu, Mihai. *Gloss*. Trans. C. M. Popescu. Retrieved December, 5 2005 from http://www.mihaieminescu.ro/en/literary_work/poems/gloss.htm

Fiske, John. *Understanding Popular Culture*. London: Routledge. 1996.

---

[36] Roland Barthes, *Criticism and Truth*, 42.

Foucault, Michael. *The History of Sexuality* Volume I. Trans. R. Hurley. New York: Pantheon Books. 1978.

Frith, Simon. "The Cultural Study of Popular Music." In *Cultural Studies*, edited by Lawrence Grossberg, 1992, 174-186. London: Routledge, 1998.

Hebdige, Dick. *Subculture: The Meaning of Style*. London and New York: Routledge, 1999.

Jameson, Frederic. *Postmodernism or, the Cultural Logic of Late Capitalism*. London: Verso, 1996.

Jones, Mike. "The Music Industry as Workplace: an Approach to Analysis." In *Cultural Work: Understanding the Cultural Industries,* edited by Andrew Beck, 147-156. London: Routledge, 2003.

Kahn-Harris, Keith. "The Failure of Youth Culture: Reflexivity, Music and Politics in the Black Metal Scene." *European Journal of Cultural Studies* 1 (February 2004): 95-111.

Kellner, Douglas. *Media Culture: Cultural Studies, Identity and Politics between the Modern and the Postmodern*. London: Routledge, 1996.

Lundby, Knut and Helge Ronning. *Media-Culture-Communication: Modernity Interpreted Through Media Culture*. Oslo: Norwegian University Press, 1991.

Marcuse, Herbert. *One-Dimensional Man*. Boston: Beacon Press, 1991.

Moynihan, Michael and Søderlind, Didrik. *Lords of Chaos*. Los Angeles: Feral House, 2003.

Negus, Keith. "Popular Music: Between Celebration and Despair." In *Questioning the Media*, edited by John Downing, 379-393. London: Sage Publications, 1995.

Omland, Atle. "Catharina Raudvere, Anders Andrén and Kristina Jennbert: Myter om det nordiska. Mellan Romantik och politik. Vagar till Midgard I." *Norwegian Archeological Review* 36 (2003): 84-86.

Shoemaker, P. J. & Reese, S. D. *Mediating the Message: Theories of Influences on Mass Media Content.* London: Longman Publishers, 1996.

The Poetic Edda. Trans. C. Larrington. Oxford: Oxford University Press, 1999.

Thyrfing. Retrieved May 2, 2005, from: http://www.metalbite.com/interviews/thyrfing.asp

Turville-Petre, E. O. G. *Myth and Religion of the North*. New York, Chicago and San Fransisco: Holt, Rinehart and Winston, 1964.

CHAPTER FIVE

FRUSTRATED LISTENING:
MUSIC, NOISE AND TRAUMA

VINCENT MEELBERG

Abstract: This essay asks of whether and in what way, if any, the experience of trauma may be represented in music. The concern is less with trauma as an object of representation, than with the structural properties of the representation itself; that is, the signifying function of music. The argument is that such an enquiry remains problematic as long as it is conceived as the mapping of a psychological state onto musical form. Meelberg rejects the notion that musical structure reproduces the psychology of trauma, whether in terms of repressed memory or the failed *gestalten*. Narratological accounts of psychology fare somewhat better in so far as there is a theoretical compatibility between music and experience when both are framed in terms of discourse. Meelberg favours an approach that stresses the temporal isomorphism of music and experience. In this way it is possible, in Kantian style, to determine the necessary conditions under which music would become a direct and immediate representation of trauma. Alas, the mania of deductive logic produces the most pristine of conceptual worlds that ultimately cannot be translated back into life on earth. Fascinatingly, the musical embodiment of trauma implies an impossible music. And so, with a pathos unusual in an academic essay, the analysis shifts from the heady realms of theory to an altogether more humble occupation: the analysis of marginal sonic material, stray granules of sound, caesuras, elements found in a musical context that resist musical phraseology.

In contemporary cultural studies the concept of trauma has come to play an important role in the analysis of cultural objects. Cultural analysts these days are attuned to the traumatic effects of violent social upheaval, war, genocide oppression and rape. In particular, the critical understanding of such traumatic experience has been applied in studies of the psychology and semiotics of war, the Holocaust, slavery, postcolonial studies and gender studies.[1] However, one has to be careful in using this concept. Too casual a usage of the term would more than likely result in an inflation of the meaning of trauma, with the result

---

[1] See for instance Van Alphen (2006), Antze and Lambek (1996), Caruth (1996), Felman (2002), Foster (1996), Hirsch (1999), and Santner (1990).

that all "unpleasurable" events might be labelled traumatic, thus overlooking the specific qualities of trauma. It is important for political and ethical, as well as, purely conceptual reasons that the concept of trauma retain its continued applicability. It is an important critical concept in the understanding of the illegitimate and self-serving use of social and political power. Therefore, it is crucial to respect the specific characteristics that have been originally ascribed to the experience of trauma.

Music studies have always lagged behind cultural studies when it comes to the development of new theory. It would be fruitful, for example, to apply a hermeneutics of trauma to works such as Krzysztof Penderecki's *Threnody to the Victims of Hiroshima* (1960), Olivier Messiaen's *Quatuor pour la fin du temps* (1940), or, to take a more recent example, John Adams's *On the Transmigration of Souls* (2002). While these works are without doubt related to profoundly traumatic experience—Hiroshima, incarceration in a German prisoner of war camp during World War II, and the events of September 11, respectively—the music itself is not traumatic; rather, it is the historically specific context that the music refers to which is the locus of trauma. It may be speculated that rather than *embody* trauma, these works *refer* to trauma.

Thus the approach in this essay is to interrogate not only trauma as an experience, but trauma as representation. There are two directions that such a study might take. On the one hand, there is trauma as representation of …, to use an old existentialist formulation. In this case, trauma is a concept or an image. On the other hand, it is possible to talk in terms of a quality of trauma that inheres in the representation itself. Here the interest lies in what may be seen as the structural properties of the representation of trauma. That is, is it possible to learn what a trauma is by listening to music? Can music delineate trauma? And if so, what musical resources are needed in order to achieve this?

For a working definition of trauma, I refer to work on memory and trauma by psychologists, Bessel van der Kolk and Onno van der Hart, who define trauma according to Pierre Janet's model as the intrusive undergoing of an overwhelming and often terrifying event, for which no framework is at the time available to deal with it in an effective manner. Ideally, such events would be associated with previous experiences in the networks of memory and thus integrated into existing meaning schemes. Thus, traumatic memory lies outside the reach of the narrative structure of memory and language. The traumatic event in this case remains forgotten, because it is not stored in an available memory network, and yet it remains unforgettable because those networks have not yet processed it.[2]

---

[2] See Bessel van der Kolk and Onno van der Hart, "The Intrusive Past: the Flexibility of Memory and the Engraving of Trauma" (1995).

This conception might be helpful in relating the structural properties of trauma to music. For example, if a listener were to encounter a piece of music that, somehow, contained musical events which resisted integration into the musical framework of the work, the music could be said to be an expression of a traumatic event. In order to further explore this hypothesis, it is necessary to make clear the manner by which a listener recognises and integrates musical events into a larger whole.

In his study into musical cognition, Bob Snyder addresses the question of how the listener's recognition and organization of the musical event is directed by the music itself. Snyder distinguishes three principles by which music can be divided into events, which he calls groupings: the principles of proximity, similarity, and continuity.[3] In the first principle, proximity, sounds that are close together in time will tend to be grouped together. Snyder regards this principle as "a primary grouping force at the melodic and rhythmic level."[4] He contends that "of all the primitive grouping factors, temporal proximity appears to have the strongest effect and can often prevail over other grouping factors."[5] The time interval between events does not have to be large, since

> in the ongoing flow of acoustical events, a slight difference in timing can form a temporal grouping boundary as well as a large difference can—it is the *change* in distance that is important. All other things being equal, an increase in time interval between the beginning of two events in a sequence will establish a grouping boundary.[6]

With regard to the other principles by which music can be divided into events, Snyder remarks that under the principle of similarity sounds perceived as being similar will tend to be grouped together. Concerning this principle, Snyder remarks that "similarity can create groupings in both vertical [simultaneous grouping] and horizontal [sequential grouping] dimensions of music."[7] Thus, similarity can create both harmonic and melodic events. And finally, under the principle of continuity, a series of sounds that consistently, or continuously, changes value in a particular direction, according to a certain pattern, will tend to form events.[8]

This manner of representing musical events implies that at a certain moment these events give the impression of having reached closure, wherein there is reached some kind of final state or a sense of completion. Such a closure can be

---

[3] Bob Snyder , *Music and Memory: an Introduction*, 39-43.
[4] Bob Snyder, *Ibid*, 40.
[5] Bob Snyder, *Ibid*, 40.
[6] Bob Snyder, *Ibid*, 40 (emphasis in the original).
[7] Bob Snyder, *Ibid*, 41.
[8] Bob Snyder, *Ibid*, 43.

a temporal interval that is larger than the immediately preceding ones, a sound that is significantly different from the immediately preceding sounds or a halt in a continuous change. These kinds of closure are created by the interplay of tension and resolution as represented by the music, and therefore, strictly speaking, are representations rather than physical entities. Hence, closure is not necessarily the same as a physical close-down. Pushing the stop button of a compact disc player in which a disc is playing can create a physical close-down, but it does not give the same sense of the completion as does the *event* of closure.

While closures can mark out individual events, it does not automatically follow that such events stand out alone in the music. An event can metaphorically cause another event, in the sense that one event "points" to the next one. There is some kind of directedness implied between events, a directedness that underpins the intuition that the specific magnitude of an event is somehow composed of the configuration of smaller units or events. One event can also resemble another event or give, in some other way, the impression that the event is part of a larger grouping. Thus a musical phrase is an event and may be construed in terms of a grouping, one that is in turn an element in the configuration of an even larger grouping, or event. In this way different kinds of closures may be represented; namely, the so-called soft closure that functions as the basic articulation of individual events, and the closure of the complete musical phrase that has more of an effect of finality than soft closures have.[9]

One of the reasons why many contemporary compositions are regarded as ungraspable is exactly the inability to hear in the music any kind of closure. In this kind of music, no individual events are detectable, nor any kind of directedness and expectations stemming from that directedness. Snyder asserts that

> in a sequence without any recognizable directed pattern of motion, any element can be the last one—we have no basis for predicting. To establish closure, especially at higher levels, we must have some basis for predicting what we think will come next. Although our predictions may be wrong, the very fact that we can have expectations creates a tension that carries us through a sequence and makes closure possible.[10]

If a listener has no expectations with regard to the music she or he is listening to, it is because the music does not represent musical events and musical phrases. No tension is created by this music, and thus, as Snyder concludes, possibilities for the representation of closure are not available. Or, to put it in the language of the theory of trauma, the music cannot be perceptually integrated into a larger

---

[9] Bob Snyder, *Ibid,* 54-59.
[10] Bob Snyder, *Ibid,* 61.

whole. Thus a musical piece that represents or embodies the phenomenon of trauma should contain one or more events that cannot be integrated in any way into the larger, graspable whole. According to this definition, for example, atonal music, while it does resist integration, does not represent trauma insofar as it lacks a larger a larger whole, and thus higher level integration.

Kiene Brillenburg Wurth follows this line of reasoning, arguing that certain kinds of music

> display or *enact* the (violent) break in the context, the paradox of the immemorial, and, in relation to this, the inability of closure or resolution that also typifies the "experience of trauma."[11]

She regards music that both represents and frustrates temporal development through its lack of closure, and therefore fulfillment, as enactments of traumatic events. By "enactment" she refers to the possibility of music voicing or staging "a rupture that resists narrative integration and, as such, resists an inclusive synthesis."[12] Such music may be regarded as a representation of the traumatic event, one that that resists narrative integration. Clearly this does not mean that listening to this kind of music is a traumatic experience. Rather, Brillenburg Wurth recognises a structural analogy between this kind of music and the traumatic event.

Accordingly, Brillenburg Wurth asserts that when events of a musical piece cannot be brought together in any way on some kind of metalevel, then this piece is said to be a representation of what a traumatic event is.[13] In order to illustrate her point, she takes a musical piece that starts off tonally, using functional harmony. She continues:

> if the tonal center suddenly falls apart within a specifically tonal setting this catches the "autonomous gaze of experience" off-guard, leaving it with little else to feed on so as to organize and control listening as a tonal, synthetic listening.[14]

Because the piece begins tonally, a sudden disruption of tonality cannot be united in any way with the tonal context, while at the same time, the listener cannot think of an alternative schema to relate the music to instead of functional harmony. Therefore, Brillenburg Wurth argues, in this case, tonal listening is the only remaining option. "As a result, the synthetic activity bumps against a sonorous matter that literally resists [being] brought into relation ... and in this

---

[11] Kiene Brillenburg Wurth, "The Musicality of the Sublime: Infinity, Indeterminacy, Irresolvability," 255 (emphasis in original).
[12] Kiene Brillenburg Wurth, *Ibid,* 255.
[13] Kiene Brillenburg Wurth, *Ibid,* 268.
[14] Kiene Brillenburg Wurth, *Ibid,* 264.

way opposes a formative activity feeding on recall, recognition, and integration."[15] Where disruptions occur frequently and where each disruption is qualitatively different from its predecessor, the recognition of the specific disruption is hindered, which leads to the fragmentation of the music. This means that after the disruption, the music never regains a final synthesis; the disruptions leave a gap in the whole of the music.[16] This in turn leads to an absence of framework, or metalevel, in which the music can find its place in order, subsequently, to be remembered. Consequently, such music is a representation of the traumatic event.[17]

Yet, it must be asked, is the absence of an appropriate style type, and with it the inability of closure or resolution, sufficient to establish such a representation? Trauma might imply the inability of closure, resolution and the absence of a framework. However, this does not mean that the inability of closure or resolution and the absence of a framework automatically implies trauma. While the claim that psychological categories may explain the structural analogy between the experience of trauma and music is in general valid, there arises the problem that it fails to explain with logical *sufficiency* the properties of trauma.

A different account of trauma, one that does not speak of mental schemas or networks, might be capable of articulating this relation in a more precise manner. Following the path set by theorists such as Jacques Lacan and the philosophers of the linguistic turn, it is possible to develop an account of trauma that focuses on the symbolic order and discursivity.

In such an account, experience can no longer be seen as strictly individual. While experience is of course subjectively lived, it extends beyond the parameters of individual psychology and takes place at the level of complex cultural networks. Experience is grounded on cultural discourses, the implication of which is that experiences and memories are intersubjective. The discourses and symbols that make subjective experience possible in the first place is also the medium through which the human subject enters into relationships with other subjects. The individual's experiences and memories therefore do not isolate him or her from others. Rather, they make culture possible. Subjective experience depends on discourse to come about, which means that it doesn't depend exclusively on the event or a history of events. Experience depends also on the discourse in which the event finds its form.[18]

---

[15] Kiene Brillenburg Wurth, *Ibid*, 265.

[16] Kiene Brillenburg Wurth, *Ibid,* 266.

[17] Listening to music always leaves gaps in the memory of that music, since it is impossible to remember all of the music that is listened to. This, however, has nothing to do with this music being a representation of the phenomenon of trauma.

[18] Ernst van Alphen, "Symptoms of Discursivity: Experience, Memory and Trauma" (1999), and Joan Scott, "Experience" (1992).

The notion of experience thus already implies a certain degree of distance from the event. As Ernst van Alphen puts it: "[E]xperience is the transposition of the event to the realm of the subject. Hence the experience *of* an event is already a representation of it and not the event itself."[19] Trauma, on the other hand, is the impossibility of experiencing—and consequently memorizing and representing—an event. This implies that it is contradictory to speak of a traumatic experience or memory. After all, experience *is* somehow discursive, while trauma amounts to the impossibility of dealing with an event in a discursive manner.[20] Thus, traumatic events are characterized as precisely those events that are marked by a lack of distance, a lack of mediation.

Just as in Pierre Janet's account, trauma is here a failed experience, an event that a human subject underwent, and which cannot be grasped by him or her. However, as has been shown, this is not just the failure of integration into mental schemas, but also a failure to render the traumatic event discursive. This is not to say that Janet was wrong in his account of trauma; rather, his account applies only to the intrapersonal consequences of trauma, whereas the intersubjective aspects of trauma are equally important, and perhaps even more important when it concerns the relation between trauma and music.

In order to further elaborate on this point, I would like to refer to Van Alphen's discussion of the Holocaust. He claims that one of the reasons many Holocaust survivors cannot give a proper account of what they underwent is because there exists the lack of a plot or narrative frame, by means of which the events experienced by the individual can be narrated in a meaningful and coherent way.[21] By "coherence" is meant the kind of order or arrangement that would enable the survivor to deal with the events, to give it a place. But because existence in the concentration camps had no precedent, it was impossible for the survivors to give these events a place in a narrative frame in a manner that would be acceptable to him or her. As Van Alphen notes, the plots or narrative frames that were available or that were inflicted are unacceptable, because they do not do justice to the way in which one partakes in the event:

> Narrative frameworks allow for an experience of (life) histories as continuous unities. It is precisely this illusion of continuity and unity that has become fundamentally unrecognizable and unacceptable for many survivors of the Holocaust. The camp experience continues, whereas the camps only persist in the forms of Holocaust museums and memorials. The most elementary narrative framework, which consists of the continuum of past, present, and future, has disintegrated ... It is precisely for [the survivors, for whom] the past of the

---

[19] Ernst van Alphen, *Ibid*, 27 (emphasis in original).
[20] Ernst van Alphen, *Ibid*, 26.
[21] Ernst van Alphen, *Ibid*, 28.

Holocaust continues that narrative frameworks that make use of the sequence
past, present, and future are inadequate.[22]

Linearity, that is, the sequence past, present, and future do not coherently apply
when characterizing the way in which Holocaust survivors continuously in the
present undergo the camp events. There are no narrative frames available with
which they can make these events discursive, and thus make them into
experiences and a part of the past.

Note that linearity does not refer to the way memory actually works, which is
far more complicated than the straightforwardness suggested in the schema past,
present and future. Rather, linearity refers to the way in which the human subject
makes sense of the world, structures his or her experiences and integrates them
into a graspable whole. Furthermore, linearity helps in creating an account with
which the human subject can make the events she or he undergoes discursive. In
this sense linearity is illusory: it is a human creation that does not necessarily
have to comply with reality.[23]

I would like to suggest that music can be said to be a proper representation of
the phenomenon of a traumatic event in so far as it generates the impossibility of
integration regarding the musical past, present, and future. When it is no longer
possible to distinguish in a piece of music between discrete musical events,
which, as I will explain below, belong to the musical past, and the continuous
unfolding of musical sounds, which is the present, then the music can be
regarded as such a representation.

What is needed at this point of the argument is a precise conception of the
musical present and the musical past. Music can only present itself in the "now,"
as David Clarke remarks: "An essential aspect of the relationship between
perception and time is that the former, strictly defined, can take place only in the
present."[24] Therefore, music always unfolds in the present. This continuing
"presence in the present" is highly pertinent to the representation of time.
According to Günter Figal, time is the concatenation of the present: "its
decomposition into different steps and stages; it is the modification of presence
into the past, present and future, and only to be recognised as such on the ground
of this uniform presence."[25] Presence is the means by which time can be

---

[22] Ernst van Alphen, *Ibid,* 35.

[23] For a more elaborate account of this process, see David Herman, "Stories as a Tool for
Thinking" (1966).

[24] David Clarke , "Structural, Cognitive and Semiotic Aspects of Musical Experience",
113.

[25] "[…] ihr Auseinanderlegen in verschiedene Schritte und Stadien; sie ist die
Modifikation von Präsenz in Vergangenheit, Gegenwart und Zukunft und als solche nur
auf dem Grund einheitlicher Präsenz zu erkennen." Günter Figal, "Zeit und Präsenz als
ästhetische Kategorien", 16 (author's translation).

perceived. Past and future can only be recognised when there is a present, a now. There can be no time without a present, no matter how fleeting and unstable. Listening to music takes place in a continuing present, which means that music acts as a perpetual supplier of temporal reference points.

While it may be said that music inheres in the present, through the presentation of sounds; such sounds are subsequently regarded as belonging to a musical event. Sounds shift from belonging to a process—the succession of sounds—to belonging to a static group, or the musical event. Therefore, at two different points in time, sounds can be interpreted differently: "a phenomenological difference which in terms of time consciousness can only be described as an opposition between past and present."[26] In the present, a sound presents itself as part of a continuing process, an unfolding, whereas in the past, a sound may be said to have become part of a musical event. Were the musical past not to exist, music could have no duration. As David Burrows remarks:

> [T]he coupling of the flow of sounds with the attention of perceivers is controlled by the temporality of the sounds, and is therefore limited to a now whose content changes ceaselessly. Music takes place in its own almost total sonic absence.[27]

The presentation of the flow of sounds occurs in the present only, but experiencing these sounds as music, and thus recognising musical events by hearing closures, can only occur in relation to the past. The contents of the musical present never persist in an unchanging continuum and cannot be retained as such in the present. In music, the relation between present and past equals the relation between perceptible sounds and musical events.

What I would like to term "musical tense" articulates a relation between the unfolding of musical sounds, on the one hand, which is the musical present, or the wholeness of music, and musical events, on the other hand, which is the musical past, or a collection of parts. The whole is the continuous presentation of music, but it is a whole that cannot be retained. Music-as-retained; that is, music-made-discursive or musical experience, is music that is regarded as consisting of discrete parts, and it is the sum of these parts that constitute the musical past. Hence, musical tense is that element of music that represents retainable parts— the musical event—in a non-retainable whole, understood as the continuum of sounds by which the music presents itself.[28]

---

[26] David Clarke, "Structural, Cognitive and Semiotic Aspects of Musical Experience", 117.

[27] David Burrows, "A Dynamic Systems Perspective on Music", 529.

[28] For a more detailed discussion of musical tense and its relation to musical narrativity, see Vincent Meelberg, *New Sounds, New Stories: Narrativity in Contemporary Music* (2006).

At this point, I would like to suggest that the musical representation of the phenomenon of trauma takes place in music that lacks musical tense. In so far as musical tense establishes a relation between the unfolding of musical sounds and musical events, that is, between the musical present and the musical past, it ensures a distance between the music and the listener. However, in music that I argue to be a valid representation of the phenomenon of trauma, this distance has collapsed, or is nonexistent. It is musical tense that makes musical events—and ultimately the musical work as a whole—discursive. Music that lacks musical tense is resistant to discursive framing. Neither can such music be regarded as consisting of musical events, for these events belong in the musical past. Consequently, the listener cannot retain music that exhibits these characteristics, nor can she or he reflect upon it.

However, there must be doubt as to whether such music actually exists. It goes without saying that a listener cannot literally remember every moment of a piece of music she or he has been listening too, but this does not necessarily lead to the impossibility of reflecting on the music. Even if the music were ungraspable and / or chaotic, it is nigh impossible to envision a total lack of distance between the music and the listener.

However, while it is not possible to eliminate distance between musical structures and the listener, I will argue that certain sounds may be regarded as a representation of the phenomenon of the traumatic event. While such sounds do not constitute a lack of distance, they refer in other ways to trauma. Overall, I would maintain that it is not possible to create, through musical structures alone, a musical piece that could act as such a representation.[29]

In order to show how it is that a proper representation of the phenomenon of a traumatic event cannot be constituted through musical structures, I would like to refer to a work by the Dutch composer, Louis Andriessen—*Sweet for recorders* (1964), for alto recorder and tape. On the first page of the score, as published by Donemus, Amsterdam in 1964, Andriessen writes the following introduction:

> *Sweet for recorders* is a piece for treble (alto) recorder solo where at a certain moment something happens, which is known in the [sic] psychiatry as a "black-out" (mental block). The soloist is incapable to continue playing, one hears a continuous grey emptiness during 1'45"; and after that period the soloist

---

[29] In my view, the only musical structure that could act as such a representation would consist of a single, uniform sound, which would sound forever and would have always sounded. As soon as a uniform sound stops, the listener can identify a closure. The result would then be that the listener would have found a piece of music that consists of one single event. In so doing, the listener would have bracketed it by turning it into an event, and thereby made it an event of the past on which she or he could ponder. The listener would have now succeeded in making the music discursive.

continues, not, or hardly influenced by his passed psycological [sic] situation (which is in this composition an auditive situation); or it should be the fact that he hardly plays new musical material, but most repetitions of previous musical elements.

Indeed, the piece begins with a virtuoso recorder part, in which large intervals and complicated rhythms can be heard. Then, at a very unexpected moment, the recorder stops and a uniform noise, resembling the hiss you can hear while playing a blank audiotape at a high volume, sets in for one minute and forty-five seconds.[30] After that, the recorder part returns, as if nothing has happened, playing a variation of the last phrase that was played before the noise entered. The piece continues with variations of earlier musical material and ends in a fairly standard manner with a distinct closure.

During the course of the entire composition, closures, and thus musical events, can be identified, the largest event being the 1'45" of noise. Within this period, no closures can be perceived, and thus no events within this period can be recognised. Hence, only the period as a whole can be regarded as an event. As a result, one could say that there is a lack of musical tense during that period. But if we consider this period as being embedded within the piece, then, at most, we can say that musical tense is temporarily suspended.

However, since the timbre of the noise itself reminds the listener of a blank audiotape being played,[31] we might consider this fragment as an explanation of what the traumatic event is: the recording of an event—the original function of a tape recorder—whose retention and communication is at the same time experienced as impossible, because the blank tape is inaudible. Hence, in a paradoxical manner, this fragment can be seen as a representation of the phenomenon of a traumatic event after all. Paradoxical, because it can be considered as a representation of an unframeable event. It is only once the listener has recognised the sound as the hiss of a blank audiotape that she or he can label this sound as such a representation. Moreover, it is because of the indexical quality of the sound itself—the sound pointing to a blank audiotape that is being played—that the listener arrives at this interpretation, and not because the fragment as a whole constitutes a rupture in the music. Thus, it is not

---

[30] Interestingly, the only recording of this piece that I could find (performed by Walter van Hauwe in 1988, released by Attacca Babel 8847) deviates from the original score. Instead of a uniform noise, in this recording an electronically altered recorder part is inserted, accompanied by synthesized sounds. Perhaps the prospect of having to disturb the virtuoso instrumental part by random noise was, dare I say, too "traumatic" for the performer?

[31] Admittedly, the title of the composition aids in identifying the 1'45" of noise as the hiss of a blank audiotape being played—the hiss is the second recorder: a tape recorder, to be more exact.

because of the musical structure, but because of the qualities of the sound itself that the listener can regard the fragment as such.

Of course, I do not want to argue that this sound cannot be interpreted in any other way. It is not the case that this sound refers compellingly to trauma. But what I do maintain is that it is possible to interpret it as such. If one wants to interpret *Sweet for recorders* within the context of trauma, the hiss offers possibilities to do so. But this does not exclude other possible interpretations of this sound. The interpretation given above, considered within the context of trauma, is just one of many interpretations that are possible.

Still, the 1'45" of noise does not seem to fit into the piece as a whole. Its character differs fundamentally from the rest of the piece, without it being announced or anticipated in any way. Likewise, the return of the alto recorder after the 1'45" also comes unexpectedly, as the noise is uniform during the entire period and does not anticipate its ending. In other words, *Sweet for recorders* seems to be a composition that is incoherent, as it consists of two incompatible parts, one part dividing the other. But does that mean that the work is a representation of the phenomenon of a traumatic event after all? The listener cannot synthesize the parts into a coherent whole, because they are so utterly different. Therefore, no appropriate style or metalevel seems to be available to the listener with which he or she might grasp the music.

Yet, the listener might be able to comprehend this composition after all, in so far as structuring processes are at play. The music can be divided into three parts, the first and the third being closely related, while the second part is completely different to the other parts. In this way, the operative structure of the piece is established, while at the same time acknowledging the work's incoherence. After all, it must be stressed, structuring a work is not the same as assimilating parts to a whole; rather, it is simply deciding on which parts are and which parts are not related.

Consequently, incoherent music, such as *Sweet for recorders*, does not necessarily have to be ungraspable, nor can it automatically be regarded as a representation of a traumatic event. As has already been established, music is not a proper representation of a traumatic event unless it lacks musical tense. And as I mentioned above, *Sweet for recorders* does not comply with this criterion. Thus, although the piece might seem incoherent, it does not lack tense. Hence, it is not a representation of the phenomenon of a traumatic event. Only the fragment that points to the playing of a blank audiotape might be regarded as such a representation, because of its timbral qualities, not because of its structural qualities.

One thing that we could learn from the above analysis is that mental schemas simply cannot be represented by musical or other perceptible structures. Such analogies almost always lead to an oversimplification of how mind and memory work. The mind is not as clearly laid out as these representational structures might suggest. Moreover, in general it is very difficult to lay bare the intrapersonal processes that take place in the mind, let alone to try to represent these in a musical structure. Instead, it might be more productive to concentrate on the intersubjective, discursive side of the mind or those of its aspects that are perceptible from the outside, such as the way a human subject communicates and positions him or herself in the world. These intersubjective aspects expressed in terms of symbolic systems are more clearly represented in music and cultural objects than abstract psychological schemas. As for trauma, it remains impossible to represent it by means of a structure. Neither its intrapersonal as well as its discursive traits do not allow for this. True to its nature, trauma cannot be framed.

References

Alphen, Ernst van. "Symptoms of Discursivity: Experience, Memory, and Trauma." In *Acts of Memory: Cultural Recall in the Present*, edited by Mieke Bal, Jonathan Crewe, and Leo Spitzer, 24-38. Hanover and London: University Press of New England, 1999.

———. *Art in Mind: How Contemporary Images Shape Thought*. Chicago: Chicago University Press, 2006.

Antze, Paul, and Michael Lambek, editors. *Tense Past: Cultural Essays in Trauma and Memory*. New York: Routledge, 1996.

Brillenburg Wurth, Kiene. "The Musically Sublime, Infinity, Indeterminacy, Irresolvability." Doctoral dissertation, Groningen University, 2002.

Burrows, David. "A Dynamical Systems Perspective on Music." *Journal of Musicology* 15 (1997): 529-545.

Caruth, Cathy. *Unclaimed Experience: Trauma, Narrative, and History*. Baltimore: Johns Hopkins University Press, 1996.

Clarke, David. "Structural, Cognitive and Semiotic Aspects of the Musical Present." *Contemporary Music Review* 3 (1989): 111-131.

Cook, Nicolas, and Mark Everist, editors. *Rethinking Music*. Oxford: Oxford University Press, 2001.

Felman, Shoshana. "Forms of Judicial Blindness, or the Evidence of What Cannot be Seen: Traumatic Narratives and Legal Repetitions in the O. J. Simpson Case and in Tolstoy's *The Kreuzer Sonata*." *Critical Inquiry* 23 (2002): 738-788.

Figal, Günter. "Zeit und Präsenz als ästhetische Kategorien." In *Musik in der Zeit. Zeit in der Musik*, edited by Richard Klein, Eckehard Kiem and Wolfram Ette, 11-20. Weilerswist: Velbrück Wissenschaft, 2000.

Foster, Hal. *The Return of the Real: The Avant-Garde at the End of the Century.* Cambridge: MIT Press, 1996.

Herman, David. "Stories as a Tool for Thinking." In *Narrative Theory and the Cognitive Sciences*, edited by David Herman, 163-192. Stanford: CSLI Publications, 1996.

Kolk, Bessel A. van der, and Onno van der Hart. "The Intrusive Past: The Flexibility of Memory and the Engraving of Trauma." In *Trauma: Explorations in Memory*, edited by Cathy Caruth, 158-182. Baltimore: Johns Hopkins University Press, 1995.

Meelberg, Vincent. *New Sounds, New Stories: Narrativity in Contemporary Music.* Leiden: Leiden University Press, 2006.

Santner, Eric. *Stranded Objects: Mourning, Memory, and Film in Postwar Germany.* Ithaca: Cornell University Press, 1990.

Scott, Joan W. "Experience." In *Feminists Theorize the Political*, edited by Judith Butler and Joan W. Scott, 22-40. New York: Routledge, 1992.

Snyder, Bob. *Music and Memory: An Introduction.* Cambridge: MIT Press, 2000.

CHAPTER SIX

THE IMAGINARY BODY IN CHRIS CUNNINGHAM'S MUSIC VIDEOS: PORTISHEAD'S ONLY YOU AND LEFTFIELD'S AFRIKA SHOX

TRISTAN FIDLER

Abstract: There are at least two ways that middle to late twentieth-century philosophy, psychoanalysis and literary criticism found of drawing the body into conceptual discourse. One was primarily political and involved critical interpretative semiotics of the way in which the body is represented in society. A second way looked in a more Kantian way at the function of the body in the ontology of representation; that is, the body as a kind of ideational element, if the contradiction may be allowed. Tristan Fidler's essay tends towards this latter consideration, exploring the ideational construction of the body within the general social environment. The forces of construction enumerated in this paper are nonsubjective and nondeterministic, nor are they purely conceptual. The concrete elements of musical rhythm—and therefore time—and the configuration of space as a luminous forcefield are construed as a kind of "armature" around which the body takes form. Fidler argues that in the music videos of Chris Cunningham there is a self-consciousness of the visualized body as a play of digital light, ideational, but real nonetheless in its virtuality. Such a body is transcendental. It is emphatic, however, that this body is not simply an intentional and abstract representation of the concrete body. This essay may be said to map out the multiplicitous pathways across which the body flickers between ideation and concretion

In music video, the dialectic between body and space expresses visually the musical tension operating within the song the video is representing. The mood of the music influences how the space will be represented through the setting and cinematography. The camera directs our view of the space in the video and, for the most part, it is focused upon a human body or bodies in the visual frame. The synchronization of body and music in music video constitutes the representation of the self. The body's reaction to the music, either in its movement or its stasis, presents to the viewing audience a medium for engaging with the song. Primarily, the self experiences music aurally, and yet the experience is most commonly expressed across the body in general, mainly through dancing. However, the music video medium can express the self through the musical body in a way that goes beyond dance. For example, the big budget spectacle of John Landis's video for Michael Jackson's *Black or White* (1991) includes a sequence where the face and upper body of one person morph into that of another, blending race, gender and age in a visual fantasy of unity, tying lyrically into the subject matter of the song. In the music video genre, the body may undergo corporeal change in relation to music, thus extending the engagement of the viewer with the musical self. There exists a tradition in music videos of bodies that are conceptualised in response to the mood and rhythm of the song. In videos like Marilyn Manson's *The Beautiful People* (1992), directed by Floria Sigismondi, Nine Inch Nail's *Closer* (1994), directed by Mark Romanek and UNKLE's *Rabbit In Your Headlights* (1998), directed by Jonathan Glazer the anatomies of featured bodies are re-imagined through design, computer special effects, make-up, prosthetics, lighting and editing to the point where they are no longer actual bodies but "imaginary bodies".

Director Chris Cunningham is a music video auteur whose fascination with anatomy remains a consistent visual theme in his work. Of particular interest in his work is the way in which the imagined body moves to the music within the parameters of the social and imaginative space it find itself in. Cunningham is a popular figure in music videos mainly because of the notorious clips he directed for underground electronic act, Aphex Twin's *Come to Daddy* (1997) and its follow-up *Windowlicker* (1998), wherein were imagined grotesque, fiendish anatomies, morphing the bearded, masculine face of Richard D. James—Aphex Twin himself—onto the unlikely bodies of school children and hip-hop dancing girls, distorting their corporeal forms to carry the disturbing undertones of the music. Critically acclaimed for the visceral impact of his images, in *Come to Daddy*, Cunningham imagines new, bizarre forms of anatomy such as the tall, thin, long-fingered alien, who, born from an abandoned television set, dripping with "goo", opens its huge, fanged mouth to scream at a little old lady who wanders into the industrial area of the video. Cunningham's imagined bodies lie between the recognisable and the unknown. We know they are not real, but within the context of video, we believe in them. In relation to such bodies, the term, "imaginary bodies" is used literally in the sense that these bodies are imagined by directors like Cunningham. However, there are also references to the psychoanalytic concept of the imaginary as has been developed in Jacques Lacan's theory of self. According to this theory, in the period between six and eighteen months of age, when the child sees itself reflected in the gaze of the other—the so-called mirror stage—what it in fact perceives is the imaginary body of the self. The imaginary body is an ideal that is distant from the self, only obtainable through its representation. As Elizabeth Grosz puts it, the imaginary body is "an individual and collective fantasy of the body's forms and possibilities of action and signification."[1] In the same way, it may be said of the Cunningham video that the image of the body taps into collective fantasies, desires, fears and anxieties associated with the body, its appearance and capabilities. Here the actualization of the self, through the body is guided by the rhythm and beat of the music, which also informs the type of space that body exists in.

Music colours the tone of the represented space in a music video, and overall, Cunningham is attracted to musical artists whose work has a dark and unsettling sound. The spaces in which Cunningham locates such mood-driven music is the urban environment—the city and industrial landscapes. Two of Cunningham's lesser known music videos, Portishead's *Only You* (1998) and Leftfield's *Afrika Shox* (1998), made in the same year, exemplify well the tension in the respective musical tracks through the situating of imaginary bodies in an uneasy relation with urban space. Neither video was a commercial success at the time of release, but their presence on *The Work of Director Chris Cunningham* DVD, which collects Cunningham's major works in music video, allows a retrospective analysis of the intense visual interest in both anatomy and urban space. The possibilities of anatomy are conveyed less through the body as a discrete entity than through the configuration of tensions within the dynamics of the spaces they occupy. Cunningham's representation of urban space explores the way in which the city environment structures the bodies of its inhabitants. Elizabeth Grosz writes that

> the city can be seen as a (collective) body-prosthesis or boundary that enforces, protects and houses while at the same time taking its own forms and functions from the (imaginary) bodies it constitutes. Simultaneously, cities are loci that produce, regulate and structure bodies.[2]

In Cunningham's work, urban space produces and regulates the bodies it houses, creating them as through a process of spatial composition. In contrast to Grosz's idealized image of the city as a boundary shared with the body, Cunningham represents this relationship as formed by anxiety and paranoia. Through comparatively different styles, responding to the genre and tone of the music, *Only You* and *Afrika Shox* illustrate the limits of our bodies in opposition to the hegemony of urban space, even as Cunningham takes the greatest liberties with his imagined anatomies.

---

[1] Elisabeth Grosz, *Architecture from the Outside: Essays on Virtual & Real Space*, 34.
[2] Elizabeth Grosz, *Ibid*, 49.

Portishead's *Only You*

Cunningham's music video for the trip-hop music group, Portishead's *Only You*, has a distinct place in his oeuvre in so far as it is in stark contrast to the shock-horror visuals normally associated with Cunningham. In comparison to infamous works like *Come to Daddy*, *Only You* is a quietly surreal dreamscape that unsettles not through visceral impact but the lingering, moody effect of its images drawn from Portishead's music. The song, a released single from Portishead's second album, *Portishead* (1997), is symptomatic of the band's distinctive sound, which has been aptly described as "evocative pseudo-cabaret pop."[3] The mood of *Only You* is one of melancholy as Beth Gibbons sings of a broken relationship with the obsessive refrain, "And it's only you who can tell me apart." The instrumentation is sparse and atmospheric, creating a tension between its dub-influenced slow beat and the suspense inherent in the use of orchestral samples that recall John Barry's thriller scores from the 1960s such as *Dr No* and *The Ipcress File*. Cunningham sets the tone and mood of the song in the darkness of a back-alley street at night. Beth Gibbons performs the song in this urban context, offering a point of recognition to viewers, while a young boy emerges from the darkness in the video's opening sequences, providing a visual counterpoint to the singer. The dreamscape quality of the video results from the ability of both Gibbons and the young boy to float in the shadowy darkness of urban space, moving slowly and surreally to the tempo of the music. Cunningham filmed both the young boy and Gibbons, who was lip-synching the song, moving underwater in a pool. Using computer graphics and digital effects, Cunningham resituated the floating bodies within the space of the street. The darkness of night becomes the medium of immersion, replacing the water the two bodies were originally filmed in. Signs of the original immersion in water remain apparent in the bleary eyes and liquid movements of the subjects, especially in the way Gibbons's long hair floats upwards, obscuring the top half of her face. There is an unreal lyricism to the bodies of Gibbons and the boy, as their movements in the darkness are accentuated by Cunningham through slow-motion photography and the reversal of the footage at key moments. Cunningham himself described the concept of the video as only a "technique" designed simply to capture "the feeling of foreboding in the song."[4] The foreboding tone of *Only You* is conveyed musically through the dub bass-line and is relayed visually in the way the darkness of the street nearly engulfs the pale skin and light-coloured clothing of the bodies, their weightlessness in space unexplained and ambiguous in the context of the video.

---

[3] Stephen Thomas Erlewine, "Portishead: Biography". In All Music Guide (AMG) website: http://www.allmusic.com/cg/amg.dll?p=amg&sql=11:oy66mpm39f6o~T1.

[4] Lance Bangs and Chris Cunningham, *Chris Cunningham*, 14.

Suturing the images of Gibbons and the young boy from their original aquatic context into urban space, Cunningham transposes their bodies into "imaginary bodies." Elisabeth Grosz suggests that computerisation transforms "an imaginary anatomy well beyond its technological capacities, yielding the fantasy of the interchangeability, even transcendence, of the body and its corporeal configuration."[5] Grosz is referring contextually to the concept of virtual reality, but her comments can also be applied to *Only You*. Here, anatomy is imagined well beyond its physical capacities as Beth Gibbons and the boy are both weightless within the space of the street. Their bodies are able to float without the aid of any prosthetic device, with both actors seeming to float on their own physical command. The boy's body hovers above the ground and moves through the air, and, for example, the moment when he floats upwards and stands sentient, clearly above the solid ground in a full figure shot is a visualization of Grosz's idea of transcendence through corporeal configuration. The flow of his movement to the rhythm of the music reflects Grosz's idea that, "there is a certain joy in our immersion in space."[6] In *Only You*, the immersion of bodies in an urban space participates in the collective fantasy of floating in outer-space, as realised by the figure of the astronaut, or in the gravity-defying aerodynamics of the fictionalised superhero.

Cunningham resituates this transcendence back into the everyday reality of the street space. The synchronization of the boy's fluid movements and the musical rhythm of *Only You* creates musicality in the imagined body, which is clearly seen in the song's bridge. Here, editing cuts between shots of Gibbons and the boy floating in the darkness are synchronized with the stop-start rhythm of the record-scratched vocal sample—"Fi-fi-fi-fi fit like that!" The staccato pace of the music is matched by a similar pace in the visual medium, undercutting the fluidity of the bodies' movements with an erratic yet energetic quality. Thus, anatomy is rendered lyrical, and the imaginary body takes flight in urban space.

In the visual schema of *Only You*, it is the darkness of the night space that constitutes the medium in which the imaginary body comes into being. The melancholy of the song combined with flourishes of suspense introduces ambiguity and the kind of tonal shift in the quality of the urban space that corresponds to bodily transcendence and paranoia arising from enclosure and surveillance. The prevailing darkness and the idea of the back-alley represent received anxieties about urban space; to walk down an unknown space is inviting danger and assault from hidden threats. Such anxiety is embodied in *Only You* by the presence of strange men who glare down at Beth Gibbons and the young boy from the windows of a tall building at the end of the street, the

---

[5] Elizabeth Grosz, *Architecture from the Outside: Essays on Virtual & Real Space*, 52.
[6] Elizabeth Grosz, *Ibid*, 20-21.

only real light source in the darkness. We share the boy's point of view towards the strange men who watch him, and in this way visual relations are established between the downward perspective of the men and low angles of the boy's upward looking perspective. In one sequence, the boy sees a man staring at him in the light of a building window. A close-up reveals that the man has no mouth. The boy pulls back in space, reacting to the strange image. While this man is unable to speak, the others are implacable, not attempting to speak, just staring unnervingly at the boy, and by association, the viewer. The visual exchange between the boy and the staring figure of a second man is scored to the suspenseful orchestral samples, which heightens the uneasiness and tension in the represented space.

Though the song's lyrics refer to an adult relationship, the figures in the video suggest an Oedipal triangle. In the video's climax, Beth Gibbons is constructed as a maternal presence by the way she begins to smile and reaches out to the boy. The boy returns the gesture, but as they are about to touch, the video cuts to the boy looking at the camera, and the orchestral swell is synchronized to the camera panning up the building, capturing three men all on different floors watching them from the windows. The camera returns to Gibbons and the boy just as their hands are parting, as if the two figures were being pulled away by the force of the space itself. A moment of connection is severed, physical closeness is lost, resulting in the boy drifting away. The men constitute the father figure within the Oedipal triangle, a role that Steve Pile characterizes as not just symbolic "of patriarchal authority [but] of all social authority under patriarchy"[7]. Their authoritative presence causes a rupture in the attempt of the boy to unite with the figure of Beth Gibbons, pointing to the uneasiness and paranoia contained in urban space.

The men are positioned inside the building looking out, and so, the domain of their power extends over the inside of the building and its outside. *Only You* explores this seemingly paradoxical but logical dimension to space: "to be outside something is always to be inside something else."[8] Though the boy and Beth Gibbons are outside in the street, they are also floating inside its darkness. Cunningham has said that the idea for the *Only You* video is an adaptation of a recurring childhood dream about asthmatic panic, walking down the street and not being able to catch his breath. He recalls that it was like standing on a sea-bed with lead boots on and looking up and seeing the surface of the water forty feet away and feeling really panicked and wanting to get to the top[9]. Cunningham interprets this leaden feeling of anxiety through a visual paradox; the body is apparently free, able to float and move, an image that stands in stark

---

[7] Steve Pile, *The Body & the City: Psychoanalysis, Space & Subjectivity*, 112.

[8] Elizabeth Grosz, *Architecture from the Outside: Essays on Virtual & Real Space*, xv.

[9] Lance Bangs and Chris Cunningham, *Chris Cunningham*, 14.

contrast to that of a young boy held fast in his "lead boots". Yet, in another way, this free-floating being remains anchored to the surrounding space. Urban space in *Only You* facilitates the transcendent qualities of the imaginary body, but it is also, at the same time, an imprisoning void. The boy can move freely through the darkness, but he cannot move away from it into the light inside the buildings. The boy is connected to the surrounding street by the way his body floats within its darkness, integrated to the boundary of space. This integration between his body and space is visualised as imprisonment by Cunningham as he closes the video with the boy floating in the dark void, curling into a fetal position and revolving slowly in the darkness. The image is inscribed with anxieties of drowning and suffocation. The imaginary body is a technical illusion in the *Only You* video, but it is also a symbolic expression of the illusion of freedom in urban space, which is imagined by Cunningham as a reality of imprisonment.

Leftfield's *Afrika Shox*

Afrika Shox is a lesser known example of the visceral imagery Cunningham is acclaimed for. While the darkness of space in *Only You* is scored to the mellow sounds of Portishead, Leftfield's *Afrika Shox* invites, in its twitchy electro-funk beat, the sound of outright assault. The antagonistic interplay between the imaginary body and urban space continues in Cunningham's video for *Afrika Shox*, which places the song in the iconic city of New York. *Afrika Shox* is an energetic electro-dance track that incorporates a haunting synthesizer melody, heavy bass, record-scratching, electronic beats, and distorted backing vocals. Hip-hop MC Afrika Bambaataa,[10] after whom the song is named, contributes vocals and a set of lyrics that reference his Afro-centric personality: "Z. U. L. U. / That's the way you spell 'Zulu'". (Afrika's name is a reference to a famous chief from the Zulu nation, the African tribe that came to prominence in the nineteenth century). Afrika's lyrics provide the cue for Cunningham's treatment of race in the *Afrika Shox* music video.

A dazed African male, dressed in army fatigue cut-offs, wanders around New York city aimlessly until, through sudden contact with people and objects,

---

[10] Afrika Bambaataa is regarded as a seminal DJ whose block parties in the mid-to-late 1970s and his 1982 single, "Planet Rock", helped pave the way for electro, hip-hop and rap's success in the mainstream. He is considered "one of rap's founding fathers". See John Bush, "Afrika Bambaataa: Biography," in *All Music Guide (AMG)*, weblink: http://www.allmusic.com/cg/amg.dll?p=amg&sql=11:ehjx7iajg7or~T1

his limbs break off and shatter. The African's[11] body is racially-coded by his skin colour, and his army fatigues and dog-tags classify him as a war veteran of some kind. The opening sequence introduces the homeless African huddled in a back street, separated from the more populated public spaces of the city. All of these signifiers position the African's body as undesired and ignored by the city. He becomes a visual symbol for the disenfranchised, poverty-stricken and displaced people who inhabit urban spaces, particularly in a diverse multicultural "melting pot" like New York city. As the African moves through the city, walking slowly and stumbling to the electro beat of the music, people ignore or steer clear of him. The African's body is an example of the post-human, human anatomy as elaborated by Sterlac, where the body is seen as "neither a very efficient nor a very durable structure. It malfunctions often and fatigues quickly."[12] Post-human theory proposes the obsolescence of an outdated and fallible human anatomy. So the African is represented through close-ups of his haunted face and in a general state of exhaustion suffered through the simple but tortuous process of walking through the city environment. In its marked fatigue and disorientation, the African's body seems on the verge of malfunctioning, by contrast with the space around him, which is organized and efficient.

The African only becomes an imaginary body through the video's central organizing concept—the racially coded post-human. The African reaches an open public space, the city square, and his stumbling movement down the steps is syncopated to the beat of the music (the first chorus is played during this part: "Let's get electrified! Let's get electrified!"). As the African steadies himself on a stairway pole, he reaches out to a white man in his mid-forties who notices him but returns his attention to the newspaper he is reading. Another white man, a businessman in a suit, walks into the outstretched arm of the African, which breaks off suddenly through the force of impact. The sound of the limb breaking, and the drama in the moment, is heightened by the cut to a flock of pigeons in the city square flying away, as if nature itself had been disturbed by this "break" with public order. The video sets up a dialectic between the African and the white men who look at him. The African is in notable shock and pain, his right arm amputated. The white businessman stares blankly at the African, looks at the broken arm, and then walks away. The other white man returns to reading his paper. The exchange of gazes in the video between the two white men and the suffering black man codes their indifference as racism. The song's title receives a layer of irony in this moment as it is only the African who is

---

[11] Note: I will refer to him as "the African" because there is nothing else that names or defines him in the music video, and because the racial and ethnic background of his body is important to the video and how the urban space regards him.

[12] Sterlac, "From Psycho-Body to Cyber-Systems: Images as Post-Human Entities," 117.

shocked by his own dismemberment. The white men are not surprised by it and, in fact, both are dismissive of his pain by their decision to ignore it. The African's body is revealed to be in crisis, subtly unwanted by both white men in regards to his presence in their space. The shock-horror of this sequence heightens in a surreal way the familiar attitude, symptomatic of living within a metropolis, of responding to public distress with apathy and indifference. The point is compounded by the following sequence where the African, missing one arm, in pain, scared and confused is seen trying to grab people on the street in a bid for help, which is presented in a distanced long shot. The sequence is syncopated to the music, beginning with Bambaataa's shout of "Afrika" and then the distorted yells of "funk!" are repeated to the beat, which the images in this sequence are cut to. People avoid the African, turning away as if he is diseased, an aspect that is furthered by the glazed, glaucoma-like look of his eyes, reminding one of the suffering people in Africa afflicted with diseases such as AIDS and needing help from major economic powers. Big city indifference becomes first world indifference to third world suffering through the symbolic presence of the African's body.

The African is an imaginary body because he has become a visual fantasy of the negative possibilities implicit in the human being's fragile anatomy. His disintegration references post-human ideas about the expiration of the organic body. Sterlac suggests that post-human strategy toward the body is concerned with erasure, rather than an affirmation, "an obsession no longer with self but an analysis of structure."[13] The structure of the video is guided by the dissection of the African's structure, the erasure of the self being the focus of the video. When the African breaks his limbs against the solid objects of the city, the broken parts are found to be hollow, which codes him as a post-human structure open to dissection without any danger of encountering the messiness of blood, bone, and meat. In the first sequence where the African breaks a limb, a close-up of the cracked fore-arm on the ground fetishises it as an object with its hollow dimensions, resembling a black piece of porcelain. Sterlac proposes that "the hollow body becomes a host, not for self or a soul, but simply for a structure."[14] The African is depersonalized by his hollow nature, a human structure not an organism. The human body is falling apart structurally, but in an aesthetically pleasing manner, where the shock of destruction is heightened to the level of abstract art. If the African's dismemberment were portrayed realistically such gore would be censored by music video television programmes, undoubtedly a consideration in Cunningham's design. It is a hollow dismemberment on both levels, where the shock of an image is privileged for its visceral power. Here, each broken limb reveals the artifice of

---

[13] Sterlac, *Ibid*, 116.
[14] Sterlac, *Ibid*, 120.

the video with its hollowness. Yet the viewer is also encouraged to empathize with the humanity inscribed in the African's expressions of anguish. The audience becomes implicated in the African's suffering, but any empathy becomes twisted by the musicality of his erasure. The dance-funk nature of the song, *Afrika Shox,* gives the corresponding visuals of dismemberment an energetic beat, which is problematic if we consider that the central focus of the video is a man's death.

The African's hollow erasure occurs as a result of his contact with the urban space of New York City. New York is both a real place but also a "major site of cinematic fantasy,"[15] particularly in traditional Hollywood musicals such as *The Band Wagon* (1953) and *Guys & Dolls* (1955). Scott Bukatman introduced the idea of "the syncopated city" in reference to the representation of New York in musicals like *On The Town* (1949) where the configuration and pace of the city is in harmony with the upbeat mood of the music. Bukatman describes such musical sequences as presenting "both an escape from the city's managerial rationalities and a reconfiguration of the city as a delirious space of possibility and becoming."[16] The American ideal of the musical presents the city as a space of opportunity where people consume the sights and sounds of the urban space as an extension of themselves. The New York of *Afrika Shox* is the polar opposite of the musical's reconfiguration of the city. For the African, it is not a delirious space of possibility and becoming. The opening shot emphasizes the hegemonic idea of the city space with a low angle crawl of a tall building towering above us, looming against a grey sky. The only possibility for the African is his gradual erasure from this urban space. Despite this, the video does not represent New York as any less of a syncopated city. The noise pollution of the city with its police sirens and voices of the crowds is incorporated into the opening beats of *Afrika Shox.* New York is still a site of energy, sights and sounds, which bewilder the African with his glazed eyes. The syncopation of his stumbling movement with the music through editing and framing, such as when he walks down the steps in time to the beat, give such uncoordinated movements a rhythm of their own. The haphazard, pained walking of the homeless, destitute African becomes a type of choreographed dance. The video's climax involves another type of dance sequence when the African hops—at this point missing an arm and one foot—into an underground parking lot and sees three men break-dancing on a mat. The video allows the viewer to compare, through cross-cutting, the different bodies, with the African appearing exhausted and broken while the bodies of the break-dancers are strong and sleek. The break-dancer moves robotically to the distorted backing vocals,

---

[15] Scott Bukatman, *Matters of Gravity: Special Effects & Supermen in the 20th Century,* 157.
[16] Scott Bukatman, *Ibid,* 158.

which include one verse that notes, "machine make the music and Afrika shock-shock-shock." By being more than human in their robotic dance movies, the break-dancers are in step with the city's syncopated rhythm, with one of them unthinkingly breaking off the African's remaining foot in a dance move, leaving him hopping on one foot, eventually to fall down. The African's fall is shot in slow-motion and matched to the echoed sample of Bambaataa's voice singing, "Zu-zu-zu-zu-zu-zulululul!" What follows is the key image of the video with the African lying on his back, stranded, with both arms (he smashed his other hand trying to break his fall) and one foot missing. Looking helpless and literally broken, the African presents an anxious image of the human body's fragility. The African's contact with the syncopated city is what exhausts, breaks and finally erases his symbolic, racially-coded, imaginary body as he hops out into the street only to be pulverized by a speeding yellow taxi. The city space in *Afrika Shox* is antagonistic and nihilistic in its affect on the body, which is portrayed as too fragile and outdated to survive if not in tune to the beat of urban progress.

Conclusion

Both imaginary bodies envisioned in the Cunningham videos have to keep moving through the spaces they are located within; the young boy keeps floating in the darkness of the alley-way and the African keeps stumbling through New York city. Neither figure has any clear purpose or destination—we are not told where they come from or where they are going—but their movement embodies the forward direction and rhythm the music moves in. The sound of the music is representative of the space that surrounds them, the tone and mood of the song affecting the representation of the urban area in the video. In *Only You*, the young boy is stuck revolving in the darkness of space in a form of inescapable limbo, a result of the mellow tone and mood of Portishead's melancholy trip hop. The nervous electronic funk energy of *Afrika Shox* propels the African to move through the city. Leftfield's violent beats and Afrika Bambaataa's guttural shouts are synchronized to the physical damage inflicted upon him. The dialectic between the body and space visually moves the music forward, propelling it to the song's eventual finish. The conclusion for both bodies though, in Cunningham's representation of the world, is that urban space inevitably defeats them. The end of the song is the demise of the imaginary body. The young boy revolves as if drowning and the African is smashed into dust. Buildings and cities represent stable structures that contrast and conflict with the perishable material of the human body. Scott Bukatman described urban space in musicals as where "the city is the song."[17] This is true of music video and Cunningham's *Only You* and *Afrika Shox*, but while the city is the song, the imaginary bodies can only dance nervously under its oppressive weight.

References

Bukatman, Scott. *Matters of Gravity: Special Effects & Supermen in the 20th Century*. Durham & London: Duke University Press, 2003.

Bush, John. "Afrika Bambaataa: Biography." In *All Music Guide (AMG)*: http://www.allmusic.com/cg/amg.dll?p=amg&sql=11:ehjx7iajg7or~T1]

Bangs, Lance and Chris Cunningham. *Chris Cunningham (The Work of Chris Cunningham* DVD Booklet). USA: Palm Pictures, 2003.

Erlewine, Stephen Thomas. "Portishead: Biography." In *All Music Guide (AMG)* website:
http://www.allmusic.com/cg/amg.dll?p=amg&sql=11:oy66mpm39f6o~T1].

Grosz, Elisabeth. *Architecture from the Outside: Essays on Virtual & Real Space*. Massachusetts & London: MIT Press, 2001.

Pile, Steve. *The Body & the City: Psychoanalysis, Space and Subjectivty*. London & New York: Routledge, 1996.

Sterlac. "From Psycho-Body to Cyber-Systems: Images as Post-Human Entities." In *Virtual Futures: Cyberotics, Technology & Post-Human Pragmatism*, edited by Joan Broadhurst Dixon and Eric J. Cassidy. London & New York: Routledge, 1998.

---

[17] Scott Bukatman, *Ibid*, 166.

CHAPTER SEVEN

THE MATERIAL EXPERIENCE OF ABSTRACTION: MORTON FELDMAN AND THE EXPERIENCE OF SILENCE

DAVID HANNER AND JOHN WALL

Abstract: This essay is a collaborative experiment. The two authors differ dramatically from each other in their background and typical approach to composition. Both authors, however, here strive dialogically to give voice to Morton Feldman's insights into compositional procedures and their artistic and philosophical implications. The essay pieces together from various sources Feldman's views on the relation of compositional practice to historically established norms, the politics of composition, modes of perception and the sonic quality of musical instrumentation. David Hanner and John Wall are careful to give proper weight to Feldman's views, tracing out in the process the latter's theory of abstract music. Abstraction, as Feldman construes it, resists intentionally the conceptual and indeed ontological norms that governed theoretical discourse in mid-twentieth century North America, resting as it does on the performative contradiction wherein the abstract is simultaneously concrete. In the second half of the essay Hanner and Wall explore Feldman's practical notion of abstract concretion in terms of the poststructuralist theories of language, arguing that the material or elemental dimension of the abstract refers in fact to the body and its function in the generation of expressive form— musical, linguistic or otherwise.

> the words are there, somewhere,
> without the least sound,
> [...] words falling,
> you don't know where,
> you don't know whence,
> drops of silence through silence.[1]

---

[1] Samuel Beckett. *The Unnamable*, 352.

I

The years of the early and mid 1950s in New York were a magical period in the history of art and music. This was a period of intersection, where all salient factors seemed to merge of their own accord, resulting in the appearance of something new and unique. Whereas in postwar Germany and France the idea that music had to have its own inner laws led to the scientific abstraction of music through serialism, composers of the so-called New York School and the artists of American Expressionism questioned older values in art, and new ground was constantly discovered in the fields of music, the fine arts and the performing arts. The age was seen as one of a radical immersion in the present and the envisaging of previously unimaginable futures.

Composers like Morton Feldman sought ways to disengage the experience of music from its representational function, wherein music had become codified into a quasi-linguistic system expressive of a set of received social and musical meanings. By contrast, music for Feldman was to be "meaningless". Nor is there any implication here, as there was on the other side of the Atlantic at this time, of angst, despair and nausea at the prospect of so-called meaninglessness. Rather, there was a kind of joyous expectation that, freed of the lexicons of constructivism, music would take a qualitative leap into the realm of "perception without precedent."[2]

Specifically the focus of attention was on the perceptual experience of music and art much in the same way that, two-hundred years earlier, the poet William Blake had agitated for a revolution in thought and experience based on "cleansing" of the "doors of perception."[3] In order to implement the idea of the pure abstract sound, music had to be "cleansed" of musical rhetoric and traditional practices of gesturing. It was therefore essential to give up the concept that music was an abstract language, so to say, and rather to understand that it had been bounded by its functions of expressing ideas or simply attracting the intellect through distinguished accomplishments of human logic.

Feldman's view on the subordination of music to cognition, and his use of the term abstract to counter this development is that "the abstract thought has nothing to do with ideas."[4] And in his 1965 essay, "The Anxiety of Art", in which he responds to the authoritarianism inherent in the teachings of Schoenberg, Stockhausen and Boulez, Feldman argues that music has become inhibited by the preoccupation with formalistic, territorial and ideational norms:

---

[2] Paul Griffiths, *Modern Music and After: Directions since 1945*, 151.
[3] "If the doors of perception were cleansed every thing would appear to man as it is, infinite." William Blake, "The Marriage of Heaven and Hell", 73.
[4] Morton Feldman, "After Modernism," 67.

This authoritarianism, this pressure is required of a work of art. That is why the tradition evolving from the empiricism of Ives, Varèse and Cage has been past over as "iconoclastic"—another word for unprofessional. In music, when you do something new, something original, you're an amateur. Your imitators—these are professionals.[5]

In Feldman's opinion, it is the essentialisation of music along the lines of cognition and conceptualization that effectively marginalises its material production, the material quality of sound itself:

> The atmosphere of a work of art, what surrounds it, that "place" in which it exists—all this is thought of as a lesser thing, charming but not essential. Professionals insist on essentials. They concentrate on the things that make art. These are the things they identify with it, think of, in fact, as it—not understanding that everything we use to make art is precisely what kills it.[6]

Feldman does not here suggest the equivalence of music and acoustic science. Nor can the experience of perception be reduced to the tandem, perceiver-perceived object. Rather, the experience of music takes place in an environment made up of the perceiver, in all his or her complexity, the immediate acoustic surroundings, the instrumental configuration and of course the music itself. Here, perception cannot be understood as a device that channels data from an external world converting it through the senses and making it available to the logical and conceptual categories of the understanding, as in the Kantian model. Perception is rather a mode of being-in-the-world, a mix of the material, social, existential and intellectual and, significantly, the instrumental.

Artists like Willem de Kooning, Mark Rothko, Barnett Newman together with John Cage and Morton Feldman made the question of perception central to their activities. Friend and collaborator of Morton Feldman, the painter Robert Rauschenberg was the first of this group of artists to make perception itself an issue through his notion of perceptional decay, which relates the parameter of time to the visual perception of a painting. Cage's piece, 4'33" (1952), was in part a response to Rauschenberg's completely white (blank) paintings and may be considered their musical counterpart, where in the enduring silence "music [is] reduced to nothing, and nothing raised to music."[7] The "white noise" of these works, antithetic to all communication theory, operates less by generating and transmitting a signal than by absorbing the acoustical and perceptional world around it. As Cage suggests of Rauchenberg's works, "the white paintings were airports for lights, shadows and particles."[8] Another very powerful artistic

---

[5] Morton Feldman, "The Anxiety of Art", 83.
[6] Morton Feldman, *Ibid*, 83.
[7] Paul Griffiths, *Modern Music and After: Directions since 1945*, 28.
[8] John Cage, *Silence*, 102.

idea of the period was that of the mobile. Sculptor, Alexander Calder, pioneered a now-familiar type of sculpture with large steel shapes that floated in the air suspended from above and so created the ability of an artwork to change shape over time. Thus the study of perceptual modes, as it is construed by these artists, proceeds by stripping away culturally accumulated representations and laying bare what are seen as the spatial-temporal characteristics of materiality; sound, colour, texture, line and form.

For Feldman, the most significant meeting that took place during this period was with composer John Cage, thus commencing an artistic association that would come to be of crucial importance to music of the 1950s in the United States. Cage encouraged Feldman to have confidence in his instincts, which resulted in totally intuitive compositions, working from moment to moment , from one sound to another, isolating material, exploring its properties, and only then moving on to the next consideration in the series. This method sounds similar to that of French writer, Jean-Paul Sartre, who, coming to prominence in the 1950s, proposed the method of "phenomenological bracketing", whereby an event, entity or instance of signification would be isolated and removed from its environment in order to be probed for its essential structures and characteristics.[9] However, Feldman never fell for the fallacy that the materiality of an event could be lifted out of its context; rather, the procedures of composition, he maintained, should simply remove from the sonic material the encrustments of received usage. Feldman wrote in his 1965 article, "The Anxiety of Art",

> for ten years of my life I worked in an environment committed to neither the past nor the future. We worked, that is to say, where what we did belonged, or whether it belonged anywhere at all. What we did was not in protest against the past. To rebel against history is still being part of it. We where simply not concerned with historical processes. We were concerned with sound itself. And sound itself does not know its history.[10]

Feldman's attempts to free sound from its historical limitations goes hand in hand with his thoughts about how sound is physically perceived. This concerns not only the body's perceptual apparatus, but also the material qualities of sound as they exist in space and time. Feldman recalls a meeting with composer Edgard Varèse, which turned out to be for him a lesson of utmost importance. Varèse stressed that it was important to "remember the amount of time it takes for the music, when first played on the stage, to go out into the audience, and then go back again."[11] Several consequences are implied in this lesson on the

---

[9] Jean-Paul Sartre, *La nausée*, 180-193.
[10] Morton Feldman, "The Anxiety of Art", 83.
[11] Morton Feldman, "30 Anecdotes and Drawings", 145.

spatial-temporal qualities of sound: First, the shift from focusing on the way sound affects and shapes the surrounding environment—the "attack of the sound"—to the material nature of sound itself; that is, the "dying" of sound as opposed to its violent and sudden birth. Second, because of the minimalisation of the sound attack, the performer concentrates on the quality of sound as it persists in time, entering and leaving the sound with utmost control. Third, and central to this essay, the quality of silence changes dramatically; as silence emerges from delay and suspension it becomes a musical parameter itself.

In order to devise a method that would allow him to explore the material nature of sound seemingly outside the parameters of received musical practice, Feldman looked to contemporary painting. In his many essays he constantly draws parallels between painting and his music. But it is not only the finished painting or composition he is referring to since he is as much interested in comparing the painters' working procedures with his own. The first painting Feldman bought was entitled "Black Painting" by Robert Rauschenberg, a large picture in which newspaper pasted onto the canvas is painted over in black. For Feldman this was not simply a collage, but something more: It was, as he puts it, "neither life nor art. It was something in-between."[12] Feldman has stated that it was at this stage in his career that he started to compose music that moved in this "in-between" state, thus generating a music that erases the boundaries between material and construction and created a synthesis of method and application—a music between categories. Feldman now projects the sound in both time and space and thereby fulfills Varèse's vision concerning the acoustic reality of sound as being the raw material of music. In so doing he further liberates sound from traditional gesturing and musical rhetoric and implements. And thus is born the idea of abstract sound.

Feldman often refers to his pieces as "time-canvases" onto which he projects sound. The temporality of these compositions is not the developmental or evolutionary time of social history or intellectual memory, with its mythical beginnings and utopian *telos*. Like Jackson Pollock, Feldman aspires to create a piece of art that has no beginning and no end. He saw a lot of European music as being heavy with symbols (the "OH, God"—diminished fourth by Bach) and memories, memories which were memories of other musical traditions to begin with. However, perception does take place in time and not all at once against some kind of neutral background. For this reason, paradoxically, the time of perception comes to play an almost mystical role in Feldman's work, combining a treatment of the past with a huge amount of fantasy. It must be stressed though that the temporal dynamic of this music is not historic, rather, as composer Stefan Wolpe once described it, Feldman's compositional technique proceeds according to the principle of "negation" due to the prevalence of

---

[12] Morton Feldman, "The Anxiety of Art", 87.

discontinuity, as sound becomes progressively absent. This method introduces the procedure of taking away musical material in the course of a piece instead of building on already presented musical material. Thus, instead developing to a climax, the piece is elongated and eventually, as Feldman proposes, "die[s] a natural death".[13]

Construing musical composition as a process of sonic erosion and decay as opposed to sonic construction is Feldman's way of entering into an almost corporeal engagement with the material. Moreover, the act of "being in the material" is in itself abstract. One cannot enter into a spatially tangible relation with the music, as for example, one can get into a car, but, as far as music is concerned, one can only aspire to be part of the reverberation of sound.[14] This notion of abstraction may seem contradictory and even malapropic. Feldman's is not a mathematical abstraction of purely formal qualities unimpeded by the clumsiness of materiality. It expresses, by contrast, the sonic and rhythmic qualities of time and space as a form of experience. If any abstraction has occurred, it relates to the separation of the musical material from the constructivist systems of history. Furthermore, despite the corporeal dimension, immersion in music is somewhat intangible. In Feldman's point of view, "abstraction" indicates this ahistorical, intangible and contradictory space, and in so doing, precludes a unified theory of composition and helps to maintain the compositional process in a kind of "in between place." "Here is my only elsewhere," quips the unnamable in Beckett's trilogy.[15] In this way, that is, by using an "active concept," Feldman avoids the pitfalls of the rhetorical concept. For Feldman, what begins as a survey of sonic parameters and their temporal organization, using both graphic and conventional notation, eventually becomes an extensive body of work, of which each piece—due to its state of consciousness—is an example of this "in-between" place designed to engage in a dialogue with itself.

In order to capture a sense for the compositional evolution of Feldman's music, it may help here to illustrate Feldman's notion of the abstract experience and ahistorical temporality by exploring some of the techniques he used in pieces from the 1950s to the 1980s. In "Projection 1" (1950) for solo violoncello, the cello part is organized in three systems of flageolet, pizzicato, and arco sounds, each of which is divided into high, middle and low registers. In the notational systems are placed squares and rectangles indicating sounds of one or more beat, which are organized within a group of four beats constituting a measure. The notation not only defies any well known musical rhetoric

---

[13] Morton Feldman, "Darmstadt Lecture—26/07/1984," 111.
[14] Morton Feldman, "Some Elementary Questions", 54.
[15] Samuel Beckett, *The Unnamable*, 370.

through the indeterminacy of the musical pitch but enhances the more immediate and physical aspect of a sound's acoustic reality.

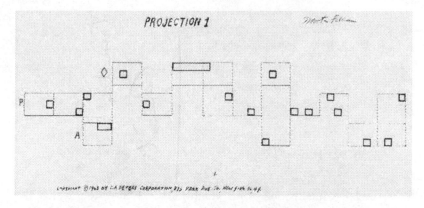

Example 7-1: First page of "Projection 1". Copyright 1962,
C. F. Peters Corporation, New York

After realising that in this way he had not only succeeded in liberating sound from constructivist premises but had also given the performer too much freedom (after all, this notation was not meant to be an art of improvisation but a totally abstract sonic adventure), Feldman developed a "free durational notation" with exact pitches but indeterminate durations of sounding events as, for example, in his "Piece for Four Pianos" (1957) and "Durations 1-5" (1960/61)—five pieces for various chamber ensembles. The group of pieces entitled "Vertical Thoughts 1-5" (1963) is in a sense dedicated to exploring the relation of musical time and real time and combines the free durational notation with conventional measures and proportional notation.

"Vertical Thoughts 1" for two pianos is an example of a composition in which Feldman tries to break the horizontal continuity, not only through the juxtaposition of registers, but by spreading chords of different structures over the entire range of the piano and instructing the performers to proceed with their next sound only after consciously listening to the decay of the previous one. Thus is brought about an apparent suspension of time. Feldman often stressed the importance of the "performance" aspect of compositional activity, which he claimed, was to a large degree an active "memory performance." In turn, the perspective of the listeners' memory performance would overlap the composer's memory performance, thereby leaving the listener also "between categories". It surely is Feldman's ideal to put the listener in this state of perceptive ambiguity and to leave him of her uncertain in regard to the boundaries between composition and perception.

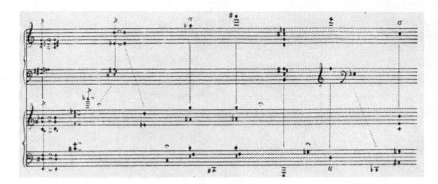

Example 7-2: Morton Feldman, opening line of "Vertical Thoughts 1".
Copyright 1963, C. F. Peters Corporation, New York

In the second and final period of his graph music (1958-1967), which always overlaps with conventional notation, Feldman expands the instrumentation and writes several pieces for larger ensemble and orchestra in which he either assigns only one register per instrument or, as in "The Straits of Magellan" (1961) and "In Search of an Orchestration" (1967), abandons the idea of separating the registers altogether and leaves it to the performer to choose. Although the measurable time is structured, the component of a differentiation in the horizontal line in this way has shifted to the vertical line, and the timbre becomes the salient factor of differentiation within the continuity of a sonic landscape in his graph music.

In 1970/71 Feldman composed four pieces entitled "The Viola in My Life 1-4" for solo viola and ensembles of different sizes. This series is remarkable for the reason that here the solo instrument plays melodic fragments much in the same way that Robert Rauschenberg used photographs in his paintings. Thus, while the crescendos and decrescendos of "the Viola in My Life" enrich the score with a musical perspective certainly found in past musical traditions, and although these features are part of the structure of the individual pieces, they play no structural role but, rather, emerge as recollection rather than from some starting premise or other. As Feldman observes, "there is a stasis between expectancy and its realization."[16]

The refinement with which Feldman escapes any formalisation, or better, categorization, is reflected in the methods used to keep the music in his pieces going. As the pieces written after the mid-1970s increase in length, one can observe that the suspension of time is achieved by stretching sound along both horizontal and vertical axes, always aware of the "breathing" environment of a

---

[16] Morton Feldman, *Bulletin of the Buffalo Philharmonic Orchestra*, 29.

sound, it is a single-tone melodic fragment or a chord. It is this basic sonic material that Feldman refers to as a "found object", as opposed, for example, to his own invention. By means of permanent permutation, reiteration, juxtaposition, overlap, inversion, reorganization, and orchestration Feldman's time canvases develop into slowly turning kaleidoscopes, reflecting the light from within.

Example 7-3: Morton Feldman, first page of "String Quartet II".
Copyright 1983, Universal Edition, London

Approaching the works from this analytical perspective and by emphasizing Feldman's very personal way of composing, a way in which he himself becomes a listener of the evolving sounds evolving, it becomes apparent that his entire oeuvre is nothing less than an astounding evidencing of the rigour and concentration with which Feldman carefully studies all the ramifications of the idea that music is an art form of sonic reality, and not primarily that of the ego.

An example of this phenomenon may be found in String Quartet II (1983), a piece that emerges four years before Feldman's death in 1987. One can observe the shading of the four-tone cluster using different dynamics, means of sound production, and timbre. Over a five and a half hour duration, the piece undergoes various states of reiteration and change, and last but not least, leaves the listener with the feeling that music can imply the infinite if enough things depart from the norm far enough. As Samuel Beckett observes, "time has turned into space and there will be no more time."[17]

II

Exploring the philosophical implications of Feldman's work is a delicate operation. Feldman is looking for a way to describe procedures of musical composition; he is not at all interested in universalising his claims. The positions put forward are subtle and nuanced and do not avail of the cautious logical conventions and sometimes paranoid rhetoric of received theoretical discourse—the syllogism, hedging bets, straw targets, misrepresentation. It is necessary to acknowledge also that Feldman's pronouncements are often informed by a project of self-mythologization. Hence, Feldman's assertions often appear philosophically naïve and thus leave him vulnerable to professional criticism. Feldman's statements about his work, however, have something of the manifesto about them, although short on polemical value by contrast with those archetypal manifestos of the European avant-garde of the early twentieth century. Consequently, it is crucial to acknowledge the performative element of Feldman's descriptive and distinctly phenomenological style. But also, if approached from a phenomenological point of view, it is possible to discern in Feldman a profound statement on the status of the materiality of expressive or symbolic form. Furthermore, it may be supposed that anyone interested in the nature of perceptual experience, sound, space and time is engaging one way or another with the philosophical nature of meaning, or signification, as it is called in literary criticism.

As has been shown, Feldman wants to move away from the idea that the depths of musical history, theory and practice contain all the forms that are needed for the resolution of musical problems, preferring instead the practice of solving musical problems at the surface. If we think about this departure in terms of Western intellectual history, Feldman can be seen to reject the Renaissance imperative that artistic material be constructed according to the norms of perspectival depth, with its field-organizing lines and vanishing-points. In contemporary terms, perhaps his insistence on surface value amounts to a rejection of the orthodoxy of the psychoanalytical unconscious as the primal determinant of meaning. Thus Feldman's compositional procedures and theoretical insights point in a new direction, let us say, away from the neurotic

---

[17] Samuel Beckett, "Texts for Nothing" VIII, 96.

model of knowledge and experience, where "meaning" is established on the basis of a set of irreducible, mutually exclusive binary oppositions, the one hierarchically more significant than the other, and thereby determinative of experience, as, for example, in the Cartesian formulation, mind-body. This new direction, from what Feldman has said, would seem to reconfigure old ontological hierarchies-in-depth in terms of surface contours so that binaries like mind-body and abstraction-materiality merge together in a way that is perhaps best explained through organic metaphors like "dance", "flow" and "tautness".

Three facets of Feldman's work, as elaborated above, are of immense interest here; namely, the refusal of historical revisionism, the implicit rejection, as we have interpreted it, of the notion that music is a kind of language constituted upon a set of precodified values, and the seemingly contradictory notion of an abstract sound that is, at the same time, profoundly material. If we consider these features as a dialectical cluster, to use Walter Benjamin's term, there crystallizes something like an ontology of creativity, one radically different from both the old Romantic idea of the inspired individual, and the "story-teller" of postmodernism.

Taking up the first point, in refusing to engage with history, Feldman and his collaborators—most notably John Cage—may be seen to be rejecting the idea of historical progress in music, wherein any particular generation would either lock itself into a struggle with history or align itself to certain, favourable historical trajectories. Indeed, John Cage argues that it is urgent that music separate itself from individual psychology, all logics of determination—including historical causality, and social space in general.[18] The counter argument to this position is that it is only by an act of bad faith that one disengages from history and society, given that all meaning is generated in relation to symbolic systems, whose primary characteristic is that they exist in social space and time. One cannot, so this argument goes, escape history, whether the latter is defined by revolutionary dialectical struggle or the self-confident elimination of impediments to what is construed as enlightened progress.

Italian composer, Luigi Nono, rails against the positions taken up by composers like John Cage and Morton Feldman, arguing that such disengagement offers a false sense of freedom and serves only the interest of the self-satisfied ego of the individual, linked in as it is with the imperialistic ends of a society, for which, no doubt, political engagement is an unfortunate spanner in the works of foreign policy and international trade.[19] According to Nono, this kind of thinking belies a Lockean dichotomy that uncritically assumes the function of the intellect—*tabula rasa*—to reflect faithfully the content and lineaments of the material world, thus leaving the initiative, ontologically and

---

[18] John Cage, "History of Experimental Music in the United States", 162–63.
[19] Luigi Nono, "Historical Presence in Music Today", 171.

socially, to the material conditions of production.[20] That which most irks Nono is the "American School's" rejection of the political and the consequent, as he sees it, obscuration of the "real" material conditions of the production of meaning. For him, all utterance, musical or otherwise, is intrinsically political

Strangely, Morton Feldman would probably agree with aspects of Nono's fierce and important argument. I say important, because of its insistence that no musical utterance takes place in a vacuum; even the most Zen-like quietism is suspended in a web of social-historical interconnections. On the other hand, there was some element of what is termed the political that Feldman felt compelled to shun, an element reflected in the absolute self-certainty of Luigi Nono's argument; namely, that the political encompasses and explicates all facets of signification, where all mutation must conform to causal explanation, leaving no room for the chaotic, the random and the indeterminate. Feldman was not reticent in his belief that musical composition must of necessity separate itself from the political. In fact, as early as 1964 he was already bemoaning the fact that his work was being absorbed into the political, speculating that "about ten or fifteen years after something new and original is done and has its first impact, that impact becomes a political one," where politics is simply the "desire for power."[21] Looking back on the 1950s, Feldman saw his apolitical past as a time of immense creativity, a time when, by analogy, he imagined, as he terms it, the presence of a kind of deity in his work, a time when he and his peers were able to explore "their own sensibilities, their own plastic language."[22] He felt at the time he made these statements that all this early work had been trampled upon by the rhetoric of criticism, the historicizing tendency and the various power games that are played out in the music world.

Feldman in no way, however, resigns himself to the inevitability of history and politics. Even if he was drowning in it, he insisted on his position. He was an artist of failure in the mould of Samuel Beckett, where, to be proved wrong by history, or experience personal failure (of the ego) was the midwife to artistic creativity. Feldman simply tried to remove himself from the din and clatter of the institutions that surrounded him, nurtured him, in order more effectively to seize on musical perception as an act of radical and random creation, neither *ex nihilo* nor woven into the golden threads of social historical time, but, as he says of his early compositions, "fresh into the moment, and you didn't relate it."[23] Nono's criticism that Cage, and by implication, his fellow composers like Feldman, had abandoned the intellect to the dangerous monster of the material

[20] Luigi Nono, *Ibid*, 172.
[21] "An Interview with Robert Ashley", 363.
[22] "An interview with Robert Ashley", 364.
[23] Walter Zimmerman, "Conversation between Morton Feldman and Walter Zimmerman," 229.

world is ill-judged. To be sure, the intellect is not central to the work of Feldman and Cage, and intentionally so. What may be found in their work is precisely the attempt to circumvent the reduction of all mental activity to the dichotomy of the intellect and materiality, as if the material were simply passive, brute existence awaiting the intervention of the intellect to elevate it to the status of reality, and as if the structure of this reality could only ever be articulated according to the logico-linguistic variations of the understanding. This is the world of Immanuel Kant, and Nono shows a marked nostalgia for the certainties of the Enlightenment. By contrast, we find in Feldman's theoretical statements a tension between the creative and, in his musical compositions, a novel attempt at explicating the interrelatedness of the artificially segregated worlds of meaning, sense, signification on the one hand, and on the other hand, materiality.

Such theoretical and musical practices bring into question the relationship between the symbolic nature of music, the character of its signifying functions and the ontological status of the material element that constitutes musical expression. Poststructuralist criticism holds that while reality only exists insofar as it is expressed through symbolic systems, most notably language, the relative fluidity of meaning points to an active, elemental, nonlinguistic dynamic. Not all expressive forms are reducible to the signifying functions of a language or code. In literature, for example, there is always something else, some residue of unarticulated desire that is, nonetheless, bound up with the processes that generate received meaning. According to linguist and psychoanalyst, Julia Kristeva, language, or expressive form, has a double aspect. On the one hand, language signifies through its systemic function; meaning is already congealed in language and individual utterances simply manifest it. Language is a hypostatic, social system, a phenomenon referred to by Kristeva as the symbolic. On the other hand, there is a creative element that inheres in language as a dynamic, generative force, termed by Kristeva, the semiotic—the embodied irruption of certain powerful drives into the sphere of the symbolic, or received linguistic usage.[24] Its locus, or site of activity, is the body and in particular the convergence of the libido and the death-drive, Eros and Thanatos in a fatal but paradoxically creative embrace.

According to Kristeva, literary creativity amongst the modernists pitched itself at the limits of experience, not as they existed, one could say, in a Romantic consciousness of depth and inwardness, but as they existed in language, reason, logic, syntax and grammar. Above all, writers sought out points of negation, not its logical function, which is judgement, but paradox, contradiction, impasse and aporia, and by incorporating them into narrative rhythm and style, all the time denying any tendency towards resolution of

---

[24] Julia Kristeva, *Revolution in Poetic Language*, 24.

logical anomaly, prised open cracks and fissures on the symbolic surface, revealing the material conditions of the production of meaning. Such materiality, in this instance, did not primarily refer to the Marxist thesis of economic dialectics, but to elemental presence of the human body:

> Indifferent to language, enigmatic and feminine, this space underlying the written is rhythmic, unfettered, irreducible to its intelligible verbal translation; it is musical, anterior to judgement, but restrained by a single guarantee: syntax.[25]

Language, music and mathematics may harden into signifying systems by expunging the body, but nonetheless, as Schopenhauer demonstrated, the material body is a precondition for the consolidation of meaning, and thereby a key element in its generation. The body referred to here is not primarily that of biology, organized into overlapping systems of nerves, bones, muscles, blood and antibody. It is rather as Gilles Deleuze and Félix Guattari would say, a Body without Organs, a region of flows, pulsations and multidimensional axes: an egg![26] In more orthodox language, the Body without Organs is a strange and incomplete synthesis of the material and the ontological. The oeuvre of a writer like Samuel Beckett, with its banal litanies and limping rhythms of paradox and impasse—"my body does not yet make up its mind"[27]—expresses the structural necessity of the material body to the ether of signification and the simultaneous absence of the body in matters meaning. This is the same paradox found in Morton Feldman's use of the term abstract to describe his music. It is at once highly abstract, in the mathematical sense, while at the same time immersed in the material or elemental dynamic of the production of meaning. Hence Feldman's notion of "being in the material", where the musical experience resonates with the kind of reverberations, pulses and upheavals that take place in the body. As Malraux said, "I hear myself with my throat."[28]

Kristeva insists that while it is only through the sleight of hand of logical antinomies that literature brings into play the generative processes of semiosis, other nonverbal systems are less bound to the symbolic and thereby exhibit a surface semiotics. She adds, though, that there is no expressive or communicative mode that falls exclusively on the side of the semiotic to the exclusion of the symbolic, although, in her opinion, music comes close to being purely semiotic.[29] All forms of expression eventually congeal into symbolic, coded form—even dreams, once they are recorded and related. This accession to the symbolic is the function of subjectivity, according to Kristeva. Here the

---

[25] Julia Kristeva, *Ibid*, 29.
[26] Gilles Deleuze and Felix Guattari, *A Thousand Plateaus*, 155.
[27] Samuel Beckett, *The Unnamable*, 182.
[28] Cited in Maurice Merleau-Ponty, *The Visible and the Invisible*, 144.
[29] Julia Kristeva, *Revolution in Poetic Language*, 24.

subject of enunciation is far from the creative impetus of meaning as, for example, was believed by the Romantics to be the case. At the locus of the subject, word, image and sound become systemic.[30] As John Cage noted, "their [composers'] ears are walled in / with sounds / of their own imagination.[31] Hence, in Feldman and Cage, the move away from the centrality of the self and towards indeterminacy. In Cage this took place in terms of the selflessness of Eastern religion—"Every me out of the way".[32] In Feldman, the dissolution of the self may be characterized by the preoccupation with the elemental properties of sound and the generative dimension of sound production as opposed to its congealed symbolic form.

The "in between place" that Feldman spoke of is thus not some vague and amorphous metaphysical space. Neither is it the empty Zen-like space beloved of Cage. It is a perception without cognition, which is not some state where perception is discovered in its pure form. Rather, Feldman insists on removing perception from the subordinate position imposed upon it by Enlightenment thought and tracing out fluid patterns and forms from which cognition in fact derives. There is a kind of musical thought that is not properly conceptual or cognitive. It is a thought process that follows the patterning implicit in sonic matter. When Feldman claims that "the abstract thought has nothing to do with the idea",[33] he is identifying his work with the semiotic processes spoken of by thinkers like Kristeva, where the body is not a thing or the idea of a thing, but a necessary condition for things and thought in the first place, and an entity that in producing thought, enters into it, but in so doing, disappears.

In the field of music, Feldman's paradoxical materialist abstraction may be further explored in terms of "silence". In twentieth-century thought and artistic practice, "silence" has played a key role. The young Samuel Beckett believed that the systematic misuse of language, semantic jarring and dissonance produced a glimpse or "whisper of that final music or that silence that underlies all."[34] Thus silence here is seen as a kind of metaphysical accompaniment to expressive form. At the empirical level, silence involves the elimination of extraneous sound, socially cluttered space and psychological intentionality. At another, perhaps existential level, silence is a phenomenon that contains in itself, implicitly, the birth and death of sound: All silence contains noise. John Cage says of his friend, Morton Feldman,

---

[30] Julia Kristeva, *Ibid*, 24.

[31] John Cage, *Silence*, 155.

[32] John Cage, *Ibid*, 171.

[33] Morton Feldman, "After Modernism", 67.

[34] Samuel Beckett, "A Letter to Axel Kaun", 172.

The nothing that goes on is what Feldman speaks of when he speaks of being submerged in silence. The acceptance of death is the source of all life. So that listening to this music one takes as a spring-board the first sound that comes along; the first something springs us into nothing and out of that nothing arises the next something, etc., like an alternating current. Not one sound fears the silence that ex-tinguishes it. And no silence exists that is not pregnant with sound.[35]

There is in Cage's silence the fluctuation of being and nonbeing, which of course is reducible to the process of perpetual becoming. The silence is thus a kind of otherness, not immediately apprehended by the intellect, but nonetheless determinative of existence. As philosopher Vladimir Jankélévitch has suggested, "silence is not Nonbeing, but, rather, something other than being."[36] Jankélévitch offers the opinion that silence is that which enables the perception of the voice of the other:

> It is silence that allows us to hear *another voice,* a voice speaking *another language,* a voice that comes *from elsewhere*. This unknown tongue spoken by an unknown voice, this *vox ignota*, hides behind silence just as silence itself lurks behind the superficial noise of daily existence ... silence reveals the inaudible voice of absence, a voice that is concealing the deafening racket made by presences.[37]

This otherness, it may be speculated is the voice of a materiality, whose most basic perceptual quality is the tension between endurance in time and the oscillation between birth and death, an oscillation that is a process of becoming, where "being" can never settle into a specific self-identical entity. In this sense, silence is a voice that belongs to nobody, as in Beckett, but also, if the terrible pun may be excused, to all bodies, where there is no self. Feldman's music traverses this emphatically elemental otherness in what may best be described as a Beckettian trope, the primary movement being the "To and fro in shadow, from outer to inner shadow. To and fro, between unattainable self and unattainable non-self."[38] And if these conclusions attribute a metaphysical position to Feldman that he would not otherwise embrace, let us not forget that music is a kind of dance, one that combines the flesh of the body with the most abstract of geometries written across the skies. After all, as we read in Ernst Bloch: "How do we hear ourselves first and foremost? As endless singing to

---

[35] John Cage, *Silence*, 135.

[36] Vladimir Jankélévitch, *Music and the Ineffable*, 154.

[37] Vladimir Jankélévitch, *Ibid*, 151.

[38] Samuel Beckett's thematization of his life as expressed to Morton Feldman in a 1976 meeting. See James Knowlson, *Damned to Fame: The Life of Samuel Beckett*, 99.

oneself and in the dance"[39] It is this Democritian dance of sonic particles that in Feldman locks together the elemental and the abstract.

References

Ashley, Robert. "An Interview with Robert Ashley." In *Contemporary Composers on Contemporary Music*, edited by Elliot Schwartz and Barney Childs, 362–66. New York: Da Capo Press, 1998.

Beckett, Samuel. *The Unnamable.* London: Picador, 1976.

———. "A Letter to Axel Kaun." In *Disjecta: Miscellaneous Writings and a Dramatic Fragment,* edited by Ruby Cohn, 172. London: John Calder, 1983.

———. "Texts for Nothing" VIII. In *Collected Shorter Prose: 1945-1980,* by Samuel Beckett. London: John Calder, 1986.

William Blake, "The Marriage of Heaven and Hell." In *William Blake: Selected Poetry*, edited by W. H. Stevenson. Harmondsworth: Penguin Books, 1988.

Bloch, Ernst. *Essays on the Philosophy of Music.* Trans. Peter Palmer. Cambridge: Cambridge University Press, 1986.

Cage, John. "History of Experimental Music in the United States." In *Composers on Modern Musical Culture,* edited by B. R. Simms, 161-69. New York: Schirmer Books, 1999.

———. *Silence*, Middletown, Connecticut: Wesleyan University Press, 1961.

Deleuze, Gilles & Félix Guattari. *A Thousand Plateaus: Capitalism and Schizophrenia.* Trans. Brian Massumi. London: University of Minnesota Press, 1994.

Feldman, Morton. "30 Anecdotes and Drawings." In *Morton Feldman: Essays,* edited by W. Zimmerman, 144-80. Kerpen: Beginner Press, 1985.

———. "The Anxiety of Art." In *Morton Feldman: Essays*, edited by W. Zimmerman, 83-96. Kerpen: Beginner Press, 1985.

———. "After Modernism." In *Morton Feldman: Essays,* edited by W. Zimmerman, 67-70. Kerpen: Beginner Press, 1985.

———. "The Viola in my Life." In *Morton Feldman: Essays,* edited by W. Zimmerman. Kerpen: Beginner Press, 1985.

———. "Some Elementary Questions." In *Artnews* 66 No. 2 (April 1966): 54-57.

———. "Darmstadt Lecture—26.07.1984." In *Summer Gardeners: Conversations with Composers*, edited by Kevin Volans, 107-121. Durban: New Music Edition, 1985.

———. *Bulletin of the Buffalo Philharmonic Orchestra: 1972-1973.* Buffalo.

---

[39] Ernst Bloch, *Essays on the Philosophy of Music*, 16.

Griffiths, Paul. *Modern Music and After: Directions since 1945.* Oxford: Oxford University Press, 1995.

Jankélévitch, Vladimir. *Music and the Ineffable.* Trans. Carolyn Abbate. Princeton: Princeton University Press, 2003.

Knowlson, James. *Damned to Fame: the Life of Samuel Beckett.* London: Bloomsbury, 1987.

Kristeva, Julia. *Revolution in Poetic Language.* Trans. M. Waller. New York: Columbia University Press, 1984.

Merleau-Ponty, Maurice. *The Visible and the Invisible.* Trans. Alphonso Lingis. Evanston: Northwestern University Press, 1968.

Nono, Luigi. "Historical Presence in Music Today." In *Composers on Modern Musical Culture,* edited by B. R. Simms, 169-174. New York: Schirmer Books, 1999.

Sartre, Jean-Paul. *La nausée.* Paris: Gallimard, 1972.

Zimmerman, Walter. "Conversation between Morton Feldman and Walter Zimmerman. In *Morton Feldman: Essays,* edited by W. Zimmerman, 229-244. Kerpen: Beginner Press, 1985.

CHAPTER EIGHT

THE SOCIAL AESTHETICS OF NOISE: INVESTIGATING THE SOUNDSCAPE OF PUBLIC ENEMY

PAAL FAGERHEIM

Abstract: In this essay Paal Fagerheim engages with the aesthetics of rap music. The particular focus is on the dynamic of noise. However, while there is much to be gained from a formalist approach to noise, any aesthetic analysis will fall far short of the music itself if the social and historical contexts of musical production are ignored. Here there is an implicit critique of the kind of musical criticism which assumes that the parameters of its discipline are coextensive with the parameters of an epistemological category. Rather, what Fagerheim argues for is a hermeneutic approach that articulates mimetically and critically the result of a musicological approach to noise with the politics (of power and resistance) of the society from which it arises, in this case the ethnic politics of the USA.

We've all heard it; music that just sounds terrible; music that provokes us and makes us feel irritated. "It's not music, just noise!" Most of us have said it in discussions about music, in the heat of a passing moment or thought it when listening to something irritating on the radio or TV. Each one of us also knows of music that we consider good, sweet, moving and comfortable with its soft and beautiful sounds. So, what about this noise that is made up of both musical and seemingly non-musical sounds? What is musical noise, and what does it signify, if anything?

This essay investigates the use of noise as an integral element in the music of the US rap group, Public Enemy. Since the late 1980s, this band has been one of the most popular and influential rap groups in the history of rap music. Records like *It Takes a Nation of Millions to Hold us Back* (1988)[1] and *Fear of a Black Planet* (1990) have been listed as some of the most important records in the

---

[1] This includes best album of the year in The Village Voice 1988, The Rolling Stone list over top 500 albums, NME's top 100 albums of all time, TV channels like VH1 and British Channel 4 and the website www.AcclaimedMusic.net.

history of popular music. One characteristic aesthetic quality of these albums is the use of non-musical elements that can be defined as noise. One of my aims here is to use musical analysis to show how such elements are implemented in the music. I also believe that musical analysis should take into consideration the social dynamic of music—music *in* culture and music *as* culture—especially its powerful presence in areas like race, ethnicity, identity and cultural difference. Therefore the analysis will also focus on links between musical elements and the socio-cultural environment. This multifaceted perspective can hopefully lead us to an understanding of musical aesthetics in its broader context. In doing this I follow a tradition of research that combines different theoretical and methodological perspectives including ethnomusicology, anthropology, cultural studies and music theory, a multilayered approach that has been more and more represented in music research since the 1980s (Middleton 1990, Moore 2003, Walser 2003).

By using musical analysis, I will point out some significant rhythmic characteristics in Public Enemy's music. The examples used here are from their record *It Takes a Million to Hold Us Back* which was released on the Def Jam label, Columbia records in 1988. In this analysis I will be partly using traditional musical notation, which is not an unproblematic approach in the study of popular music. The musical notation system shows written representations of the music, wherein rhythmic, melodic and harmonic elements are abstracted and reduced to text. The problem is that it does not show the important elements of a musical *performance*. Nor does it show discrepancies in rhythm, timbre, sound and tone colour. Nonetheless, notation proves itself useful here. Rap producers tend to arrange and layer rhythmic beats digitally as looped patterns that succeed each other identically. Drum parts, bass and other parts in these songs are often programmed and *locked* to such a looped pattern. The rhythmical complexity of such music may therefore be well represented in the traditional notation system. But the system is less suitable when applied to analysis of the rap text performance which occurs simultaneously with the beat. One of the most important factors of a rapper's performance is her or his ability to *flow*. Flow may be seen as the personal rhythmic presentation of the rap text over the beat—flow is about playing with the rhythm, following the beat but always keeping a "relative attitude" towards it. Rappers often abandon the strict pulse or metre which the beat is constructed upon. Rappers may (as in other popular music forms) perform their rhythm either stressing the beat to create a sense of forward, horizontal energy, or they may have a more laidback style behind the pulse to create another type of relaxed and unstressed flow.[2] It is this that creates rhythmic tensions and musical value that is unique to rap music aesthetics.

---

[2] A characteristic feature then of rap music, is the combination of locked rhythm patterns and loops, and performance of text relative in time to such a background.

The voice quality of the rapper is also a very important element in rap music. As for most popular vocal music, the voice gives personality to the song or the band. It is also used actively to stress the content of lyrics and the overall message in the music. This dimension cannot be well represented in traditional musical notation, but it is an important and meaningful value in the musical performance. Rap itself cannot be defined as song or by a singing technique, but it is closely related to singing because of its rhythmic nature. It also has a lyrical element expressed in word juxtaposition. Rap also demands a specific use of the voice that differs from ordinary speech. Rappers tend, for example, to bind together words and sentences in a song-like, musical manner, and they also tend to stretch certain vocals with more resonance than ordinary speech. But analyzing rap as a vocal genre is problematic and we do not have established methods in this respect. In order to fully comprehend this dimension in the analysis presented below, descriptions about the vocals are given, but should also be complemented by listening to the examples by the reader. In addition to musical elements, rap producers often combine samples of previously recorded material—non-musical sounds, guitars, bass, horns, and so on. Sometimes such samples are noise elements that seemingly have nothing to do within a musical setting. But in the musical soundscape they can be integrated as important and meaningful elements.

However, the identification of musical characteristics alone is not enough to give us a comprehensive understanding of their specific use. In order to obtain this, we need to turn to a socio-cultural analysis that can provide links between the musical material and sociological and cultural activity. This is what in my view gives musical analysis its relevance. In this context, I will focus on the historical and cultural situation in the US, especially on ethnic relations between white and black people from the late 1960s through to the 1980s. However, before analyzing a specific musical example, we must try to reach a working definition of the concept of "noise" and briefly look at the use of noise in different musical genres. I will also use some general examples from jazz and rock, and give a short introduction to the history of rap music before the analysis.

As it is used in this essay, the term noise refers to unorganized sounds that are not intentionally or consciously produced for use in a musical context. A common definition of noise is "unwanted sound", but as we deal with noise in popular music, these sounds are not unwanted; rather, they are appreciated and used to signify a special set of meanings. The unwanted-sound definition is also problematic because it implies a subjective interpretation in so far as it is always wanted or unwanted for a particular subject. A noisy sound may be appreciated by one person in one context, but regarded as a disturbing and unwanted element in a different context. Drummer and electronic-music intellectual,

Brady Cranfield, points out the relation between noise aesthetics and social contexts:

> Noise does not simply exist in and of it self, but in terms of a network of relationships, in contexts and uses: it is at once sensual and particular as well as abstract and universal. Thus, despite any occasional concrete manifestos, like disturbances on a telephone line or the use of sampled vinyl crackle for texture in a pop song, what this conveys is that noise is in some important way social in character, and, further, that noise is also therefore an issue of aesthetics. Even an apparent purely technical definition of noise reveals a social and an aesthetic quality of this sort.[3]

As has been stated by Swedish landscape architect, Björn Hellström, the discussion of noise in society is not new. Hellström posits the beginning of the last century and the Italian futurist movement as a starting point for noise aesthetics in western art.[4] Futurism was an ideological movement that included architecture, painting, music, sculpture, film and poetry, and which got its subject matter from the urban and industrial environment. As a movement, it expressed "extreme views on politics and society."[5] Italian futurist, Luigi Russolo became known for his sound machines that produced noise, and he toured Europe with a whole orchestra playing on his own instruments. He wanted to "orchestrate urban sounds" and believed that traditional musical instruments couldn't fulfill "the needs for musical expression."[6] The futurist movement influenced modern composers such as Edgard Varèse and John Cage, to name a few. Cage writes in his book, *Silence,* that

> wherever we are, what we hear is mostly noise. When we ignore it, it disturbs us. When we listen to it, we find it fascinating. The sound of a truck at fifty miles per hour. Static between the stations. Rain. We want to capture and control these sounds, to use them not as sound effects but as musical instruments. … If this word 'music' is sacred and reserved for eighteenth and nineteenth-century instruments, we can substitute a more meaningful term: organization of sound. [7]

Noise cannot then be treated as an audible entity that exists in itself, or as something unwanted. Noise carries as a mediator of qualitative information, aesthetic possibilities and the potential to become something other than what it is. Hellström gives a good example of this in relation to the content in a documentary film. A sequence in the film was taken from the back of a car,

---

[3] Brady Cranfield, "Producing Noise", 44-45.
[4] Björn Hellström, *Noise Design*, 10-12.
[5] Björn Hellström, *Ibid*, 88.
[6] Björn Hellström, *Ibid*, 10.
[7] John Cage, *Silence*, 3.

showing a road sign with the following information: "No blowing horn except for danger". Horn blowing by car drivers is normally regarded as noise. But the meaning of this sign changed when the famous trumpet player Miles Davis suddenly appeared in the same car as the cameraman. In this new context, the sign may be read like: "No blowing horn except when knowing why."[8] As designated by the term *danger*, noise is acceptable when a situation demands it; in this case, the avoidance of a car crash or the necessity of calling attention in a certain traffic situation.

In the context of this essay, we should also mention some of the specific aesthetic qualities that characterize the trumpet playing of Miles Davis, who has been appreciated as one of the most significant jazz musicians since the 1950s. Davis's playing has been criticised for its perceived lack of purity and technical brilliance.[9] Davis often missed notes and made noisy "cracks" with his trumpet. But by doing so, he accepted that his own technique, musical personality and socio-musical tradition demanded just such an audible approach; the meanings of his musical phrases were created and mediated through the use of noise elements that were regarded as unwanted from a institutionalised western point of view, which regards tone control, perfect pitch, clarity of intonation and accuracy as prime aesthetic elements in musical performance. Expressed in this aesthetic norm, and Miles Davis's encounter with it, is a significant element of cultural difference, especially that difference between black African American cultural practices, and white Euro-American practices. I will take this discussion further towards the end of this essay.

What we hear as noise then, is consequently dependent on the situation in which the sound is presented to us. Sounds are given different meanings in different contexts. Noise, then, may be seen as the production of non-musical sounds that can potentially take on a musical character in a certain context. At this point we should differentiate between two aspects of the term noise. It may also be the product of sounds produced by traditional musical instruments, sounds which are distorted and / or made "noisier". This is another aspect of the term noise in music. In popular music this aspect had several significant developments during the twentieth century, especially in relation to African American cultural practices.

Noise in Jazz and Metal

At The Cotton Club in New York in the 1930s to 1940s, the American bandleader Duke Ellington and his musicians used blowing techniques, mutes

---

[8] Björn Hellström, *Noise Design*, 12.
[9] Robert Walser, "Out of Notes: Interpretation and the Problem of Miles Davis", 343-365.

and sound effects to produce a special sound for which the band became known. Ellington's trumpeter, Bubber Miley, was one of the first musicians to develop this famous *growl* technique which eventually became a signature sound of Ellington's band. The growl was produced when Miley played the trumpet and at the same time made vibrations and sounds in his throat, cheeks, and lips. As years went by, the technique became more varied and complex. At the Cotton Club, the band played "exotic" music, which was supposed to refer to jungle sounds, Africa and a tribal exoticism. The distortion of tones in the music was then a means for reference and a symbol of another place. These seemingly unwanted and "impure" sounds became pleasurable sounds in the entertainment industry, copied by many players and bands and developed into an integral aesthetic quality that the musicians had to learn.

Another example of the prevalence of noise, may be found in the development of aesthetic preferences and norms in rock music, especially heavy metal and related genres. In these genres we can follow a development that moves from the aesthetics of clean sound and perfect pitch to preferences for more noisy elements. The guitar during the early days of blues, jazz and rock'n'roll became an important instrument in such music. In the 1960s several bands used guitars and guitar amplifiers to experiment with timbre and sound distortion. As Robert Walser observes, "the most important aural sign of heavy metal is the sound of an extremely distorted guitar."[10] Distortion had in the past been for record producers, radio producers and musicians an unwanted sound quality, but during the 1960s it became a desired element in rock. The distortion of guitar signals is created through the overdrive of power which is sent through the amplifier. The result is a signal that for the amplifier, is impossible to reproduce purely and it thus becomes distorted and significantly changes in character and sound quality:

> Despite its previous status as noise, at this historical moment such distortion was becoming a desirable sign in as emerging musical discourse … But, it is only at a particular historical moment that distortion begins to be perceived in terms of power rather than failure, intentional transgression rather than accidental overload—as music rather than noise. [11]

Noise produced by distortion became a preference in metal. One of the qualitative innovations of this process is the so-called power chord, a chord consisting of intervals like fifths or fourths played on the lower strings of the guitar. The major or minor third was at first mostly omitted in power chords, since these tones tended to make the sound too tight. Distortion enables the sustaining of such power chords, which means that once they are hit on the

---

[10] Robert Walser, "Running with the Devil," 41.
[11] Robert Walser, *Ibid*, 42.

strings, they sound nearly indefinitely. A note or a chord struck on an acoustic guitar will lose its amplitude within seconds, while a distorted power chord is sustained over a much longer period of time. The vocal timbre in metal is another element which is related to distortion and noise in popular music. At the same time that power chords and distortion became preferable, scream-like vocals, shouts and vocal distortion became aesthetic qualities, suggesting "intensity and power".[12] In the 1980s, heavy metal was an important influence on other popular music genres. Metals power chords and screaming vocals had the capacity of evoking rebellion, danger, transgression, intensity and excitement. Eddie van Halen's guitar solo contribution on Michael Jackson's "Beat It" (1982), Aerosmith's collaboration with Run D.M.C on their hit single "Walk This Way" (1983) are just a few examples of this.

Bring the Noise

Rap music developed along with the hip hop culture which arose in the United States during the 1960s and 1970s. The music has its roots in a combination of African oral traditions and African American music traditions like gospel, blues, R & B and funk. The DJ technique used by rap performers was developed by DJs in New York in the late 1970s and came mainly from Jamaican musical traditions like dub and talk-over. Dub and talk-over have their roots in Jamaican reggae and a particular use of sound systems. DJs from Jamaica, like Kool Herc, brought this tradition to New York, and other DJs, like Grandmaster Theodore, Grandmaster Flash and Afrika Bambaataa merged these traditions with new technology, dance traditions and a new sense of black pride in the urban ghettoes of big US cities. The first recordings we have of early rap date from 1978-1979, recorded by Sugar Hill Gang for Sugar Hill Records. *Rapper's Delight* was their first hit and was released on this label by producer Sylvia Robinson. The song instantly became a big hit all over the United States and then in Europe after a couple of weeks. As an integral part of hip hop culture, rap is also linked to other hip hop elements like graffiti, break dance and DJ-ing.

Hip hop itself is a term which means attitude, lifestyle and a way of living, being true to your self and your neighborhood, while the term rap covers the music of hip hop culture. Rap mixed African-American oral, dance and music traditions, and cultural traditions from the island of Jamaica with new technological and instrumental innovations, especially digital sampling and the turntables, which came to be used as a performing instrument. The DJs eventually used several difficult and demanding techniques on the turntable, making of it a virtuoso instrument. On the west coast of the USA, rap soon

---

[12] Robert Walser, *Ibid*, 45.

became a popular musical genre. In Los Angeles there were social, ethnic and political conflicts that inspired rap groups like N.W.A (Niggaz With Attitude) to create their own kind of rap music—often called gangsta rap. The early west coast style of the 1980s had its own beat: slow, cool, laidback, with a bass-heavy beat and sound samples taken directly from the noise of the streets. Cars, police sirens, screaming and gunshots were regular background noises behind lazy raps about street and gang life, police conflicts and drive-by shootings. The situation of cultural conflict announced a stronger focus in popular music. The deploying of sounds from the "hood" that weren't musical became more and more common. It also made references from local places and media audible in the music in a way that was new to contemporary popular music.

Public Enemy was one of the most influential rap groups to come to prominence in the New York of the mid 1980s. The group was founded by the lead rapper Chuck D (Carlton Douglas Ridenhour) and Hank Shocklee in their association with Long Island's Adelphi University college radio. Ridenhour and Shocklee were in charge of mixing tracks for the college station during 1982-1983. They soon came in contact with Flavor Flav (William Drayton) who joined the radio team. They started mixing hip hop tapes that were mainly broadcast on the college radio, WBAU, among them the track "Public Enemy No. 1". The name of the song soon became the name of the group, which, in 1987, signed with Rick Rubin's Def Jam Records. The group grew bigger and was joined by Professor Griff (Richard Griffin) and DJ Terminator X (Norman Rogers) and a background line-up consisting of four dancers named "The Security of the First World". Their debut album, *Yo! Bum Rush The Show,* which was released in 1987, had clear links to the music of Run D.M.C. It was simple, funky and had stripped beats that mostly consisted of "synthetic" Roland TR-808 drum machine samples and an old-school, on-beat rapping with small synthesizers, bass and sound samples. Their next album, *It Takes a Million to Hold us Back,* was released in 1988 and became even more popular than the first release. The lyrics of this album clearly state their attitude towards contemporary American society, politics, racism and social differences. The group used music to ask questions about society. However, in its role as public critic, Public Enemy gained an image and ethos associated with "guns 'n' violence", aggressive Black Nationalism and attitudes often seen as anti-Semitic, homophobic and misogynist.

The Public Enemy song "Bring the Noise" consists of a complex basic beat. The tempo of the song is approximately 100 beats per minute. At the beginning of the song, we hear a sound sample of Martin Luther King saying "too black, too strong, too black, too strong". After this, a four-bar intro comes in on a stressed and complex introductory beat, with drums and sax samples accompanying Flavor Flav. The verse starts with Chuck D rapping over the beat represented in example 8-1.

Example 8-1: Public Enemy, "Bring the Noise". Transcription of beat, verse 1

This beat consists of different drum samples combined in a complex pattern which are then looped 8 times during the verse. The transcription shows the two first bars in the beat. Throughout the first verse small changes and variations occur, but the main structure through the verse is based on these two bars. The bass drum part shown at the bottom of the transcription marks the first beat in every bar. In addition it marks a syncopated rhythm at the end of each bar that contributes to the forward and stressed drive in the basic rhythm. The rhythm is doubled in the sampled bass and saxophone voices. The snare 2 drum mainly stresses the second and the fourth beat in each bar, creating a stable and balanced element in relation to the bass drum. The snare 1 drum is higher in pitch and stresses a syncopated rhythm together with the hihat. This element makes the rhythmic environment much more complex and makes a forward push and drive in the beat. This rhythmical element is related to the syncopated bass drum but performed in double tempo. The hihat has a specific rhythmic pattern which is held throughout the entire song. The pattern is 3+3+2+3+3+2 in one bar. This grouping of 3 against 2 in the basic beat makes the rhythm of the beat more complex and syncopated. Another important element in this beat is the sound called siren in the transcription. This is a noisy, stressful and rather uncomfortable sound that further complicates the rhythmic soundscape. It is not entirely connected to the beat pulse but approximately stresses 5 beats against four. The tonal pitch is also indeterminate. This is a very important element of the song. First it makes the rhythmic feeling stressed, uneven and unstable. Secondly it does not relate to the harmonic centre of the song, which is F sharp minor. This tonal centre is mainly given through the bass and sax samples, but is blurred with the siren sample, making the harmonic landscape difficult to identify. The beat on the chorus of the song differs from the verse with more focus on scratching as a rhythmic element. Sax samples and voice samples also contribute to make the sound noisier and more complex, understating the lyrics, as shown in Example 8-2.

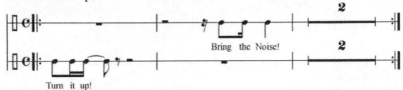

Example 8-2: Public Enemy, "Bring the Noise". Refrain, lyrics and rhythm

The drum break which starts on verse two differs from verse one in that it is more aggressive and syncopated. This is possibly done because of a shift in focus from a complete sound to only vocal and drum beat for the first four bars on verse two. The first beat then returns after that.

Example 8-3: Public Enemy, "Bring the Noise" Drum break beat, bar 1-2, verse 1

As we see, the two snare drum samples are stressing the beat with tight syncopations before and after beat 1, 3 and 4. The bass drum sample consists of 16 beats per bar, making a powerful and hard hitting bottom in the beat. The rhythmic presentation of the lyrics is in my view as important as the content of the lyrics. Chuck D makes different rhythmic accentuations, variations and syncopations over the beat, making the overall rhythmic landscape more complex and stressful. Chuck D's rap is notated on the top stave and Flavor Flav notated on the second. There we see specific words and letters that are highlighted through a doubling of both rappers, a very common technique in rap music. This results in a stronger focus on certain aspects of the lyrics.

Example 8-4: Public Enemy, "Bring the Noise". Lyrics from verse 1

Verse 1 starts with the question, "how low" black people can go, with an implied critique against the high number of death penalties handed out to black Americans. The lyrics are also filled with comments directed towards the police, here referred to as "five-o", and their attitude that to be black is to be criminal. There is also a reference to Louis Farrakhan, the black leader of Nation of Islam, which is a religious and socio-political organization in the US, founded in the 1930s by Wallace Fard Muhammad.

The rhythm of verse 2 is significantly different from that of verse 1. Chuck D starts with a triplet pickup and continues with the triplet feel almost throughout the entire verse. In bar six he alters the rhythm with strong accentuations on beats 1, 2, 3 and 4. But the words are naturally grouped in threes creating a polyrhythmic effect only with the odd combination of a specific word grouping and an accentuation that differs from the more natural grouping. Also, if we compare Examples 8-3 and 8-5, we see that each triplet in the vocals of verse 2 also occurs simultaneously with four kicks per beat in the bass drum. This rhythmical combination of several rhythms may be viewed as one of the most characteristic features of African American music. Even if this part of the song only consists of vocals and drum samples, it is one of the most aggressive, driving and intense parts of the song. The lyrics are, as is the music itself, filled with double meaning. The issues are focused on corruption, references to black soul music and criticism against Public Enemy's music. The lyrics bring a verbal message about black resistance, strength, power and cultural noise.

Music as cultural noise

To understand the noise elements and the noisy soundscape in the music of Public Enemy as cultural noise, we have to consider the social and cultural conditions in the US at the time that the music was created. Some important factors about differences between black and white cultures in the US must be taken into consideration, as pointed out by Robert Walser (2003) in his analysis of Ice Cube's, *When Will They Shoot?* from the album *The Predator* (1992). In the 1980s, the child mortality rate in the US was twice as high for blacks as it was for whites. In addition, twice as many black children as white children lived on the poverty line. Between 1965 and 1990 the unemployment among black people increased fourfold. During the same time period, unemployment rates remained unchanged for the white population. The violent crime rate was in this period very much the same among white adolescents as it was amongst black adolescents, but three times as many black youths were arrested. This fact is quite thought provoking when we take into account the fact that Afro Americans make up only 13 percent of the population in the US. Also, 13 percent of all drug abusers in the US are black, while 43 percent of all persons convicted for drug-related crimes are black. It is instructive that 78 percent of all time served in fulfilment of such sentences is served by blacks.[13] If we take such facts into consideration, we are more competent to understand the music and its use of noise elements, and also see how it can play an important role in the society. These statistics bring to mind a society that puts stress on the black population, which suggests that the rights of black Americans are not being respected. There are major differences in how black and white Americans are treated in their

---

[13] Robert Walser, "Popular Music Analysis", 32.

society. These inequitable social and cultural conditions make up the basis of rap music; those who produce and identify with such music are not in harmony or in "rhythm" with the total society. Many black Americans are fighting against the injustices of the system and have problems being heard. Music can be a powerful tool in such a situation, if used properly. The statement is clear: "Turn it up, bring the noise!" The element of social critique is musically clear in so far as it is embodied through a complex strategy of noise elements, sampling, syncopated beats and a low, bass-focused and threatening rap vocal.

A formal analysis of the structural aspects in music can explain certain of its properties. But also important is context, which is to be found in attributes like locality—where the music is created, used and mediated. The meanings and values of music can be found in this social context. Therefore it is not enough to focus on musical structure and noise elements in themselves. Rather, the relation between musical and cultural noise must be the main focus of analysis. Some key questions at this point are: Do musical essentialist parameters create cultural noise, or, conversely, does cultural noise create musical essentials? Whichever way this question is answered, it is important to take into account the nature of these creative processes? The first thing to take into account in formulating an answer to these questions is that musical codes must be mediated through symbols and rituals. In the context of music, rituals can, for example, refer to habits and norms of listening to music, the culture of live performances and, in one way or another, the extent to which the music in question is used as a means to another goal. But the musical ritual does not occur in isolation. Popular music changes and is *affected* constantly as the society around it changes. In the same way, society constantly changes and is constantly affected by the changes that occur in popular music.

Music is a powerful vehicle for social empowerment and is a marker for cultural and ethnic identity. As early as the ancient Greek philosophers, music was considered a very powerful tool in the upbringing of children. It was thought that music's capacity to stimulate the right sort of social interactions among young people, especially during sports events, was profound. The Greeks theorized that musical elements such as melody and rhythm had qualities that influenced the listener's soul and mind. The notion that music is a powerful art and has the ability to create certain kinds of behaviour is an old one and is still very much present to contemporary society.

In the early days of the twentieth century, jazz was the kind of music that it was forbidden to play in certain places. It was regulated by the white man's law. With the rise of hip hop culture, rap concerts were also heavily regulated in the United States, for example through the use of insurance regulations. Bands were often denied the possibility to play at large arenas because no insurance companies would be connected to this kind of music and the expressional behaviour of black audiences. Concert arrangers had to refuse such concerts because of the economics of the situation; insurance companies had just too high demands for them to manage. Tricia Rose points out that in the year 1990, "insurance companies who still insure rap concerts have raised their minimum coverage from about $500,000 to between $4 and $5 million worth of coverage per show."[14] Rap concerts have also suffered under politics that forbid obscenities in language and image use in these concerts. When Dr. Dre, Eminem, Ice Cube and Snoop Dogg arranged the *Up in Smoke Tour* in 2000, the show was stopped in several states because of the use of obscene film clips containing violence and shooting scenes from a liquor store, naked prostitutes and positive attitudes towards drug usage.

Final Thoughts

In the musical analysis component of this essay, I used musical transcription as a method for showing the complex rhythmic strategies in the music. But small variations occur throughout the song under analysis which cannot be represented here. A full analysis should therefore include a more complete transcription than the one I have offered here. This essay must then be seen as an example of how one can conduct a musical analysis based on both musicological and ethnomusicological methods. The same applies to the lyrics. But as we listen to the lyrics, Public Enemy gives us an intellectual and direct critique of American society. The song deals with the ideologically constructed myth of the threatening African American who is considered too black, too strong, too much in thrall to guns and dope. As the song proceeds it criticizes the songs of Elvis Presley (is he the king of Rock 'n' Roll?), the Beatles, the death penalty, corruption and the profit white America has extracted from the exploitation of African American culture.

We, the writer of this paper and his peers, also have a strong message to black society. Public Enemy cultivates a militant, nationalistic point of view in order to express the political, cultural and social malaise that is the everyday lot of many black Americans. This song can be seen as a celebration of African Americans and their ethnic identity. So, if they are to be identified with their musical expression as "cultural noise", so be it. Turn it up, bring the Noise.

---

[14] See William Eric Perkins, *Droppin' Science: Critical Essays on Rap Music and Hip Hop Culture*, 244.

References

Baker Jr., Huston A. *Black Studies: Rap and the Academy.* Chicago: The University of Chicago Press, 1993.

Cage, John. *Silence.* Middleton, Connecticut: Wesleyan University Press, 1995.

Conyers Jr, James L. *African American Jazz and Rap: Social and Philosophical Examinations of Black Expressive Behavior.* Jefferson: McFarland & Company, 2001.

Cranfield, Brady. "Producing Noise: Oval and the Politics of Digital Audio." In *Parachute 107: electrosounds.* (2002): 42-51.

George, Nelson. *Hip Hop America.* Harmondsworth: Penguin Books, 2000.

Hellström, Björn. *Noise Design; Architectural Modeling and the Aesthetics of Urban Acoustic Space.* Stockholm: Bo Eyeby Forlag, 2003.

Larkin, Colin, ed. *The Encyclopedia of Popular Music.* London, Palgrave Macmillan, 1998.

Lynton, Norbert. *The Story of Modern Art.* London: Phaidon Press, 1989.

Middleton, Richard. *Studying Popular Music.* Philadelphia: Open University Press, 1990.

Moore, Allan F, ed. *Analyzing Popular Music.* Cambridge: Cambridge University Press, 2003.

Perkins, William Eric, ed. *Droppin' Science: Critical Essays on Rap Music and Hip Hop Culture.* Philadelphia: Temple University Press, 1996.

Potter, Russell A. *Spectacular Vernaculars: Hip-Hop and the Politics of Postmodernism.* Albany: State University of New York Press, 1995.

Rose, Tricia. *Black Noise: Rap Music and Black Culture in Contemporary America.* Middletown, Connecticut: Wesleyan University Press, 1994.

Walser, Robert. "Running With the Devil: Power, Gender and Madness." In *Heavy Metal Music.* Hanover: Wesleyan University Press, 1993.

———. "Out of Notes: Signification, Interpretation and the Problem of Miles Davis." In *Jazz Among the Discourses,* edited by Krin Gabbard & James P. Lester, 343-365. Durham: Duke University Press, 1995.

———. "Rhythm, Rhyme and Repetition in the Music of Public Enemy." In *Ethnomusicology: Journal of the Society of Ethnomusicology* 39 No 2 (1995): 193-217.

———. "Popular Music Analysis: Ten Apothegms and Four Instances." In *Analyzing Popular Music,* edited by Allan F. Moore. Cambridge: Cambridge University Press, 2003.

Discography

Public Enemy (1988). *It Takes a Nation of Millions to Hold us Back,* 542 423-2.

———— (1990). *Fear of a Black Planet*, 523 446-2.
Ice Cube (1992). *The Predator*, 2435 43339-2.

LIST OF CONTRIBUTORS

İbrahim Beyazoğlu comes originally from Nicosia. He took his MA from Eastern Mediterranean University with a thesis on the influence of Old Norse mythology on contemporary culture. Upon graduation, İbrahim pursued a freelance writing career, but for the time being, conditions have necessitated that he perform his mandatory duty for the National Security Forces. When released by the army, he will resume a research project linking British Heavy Metal, contemporary mythology and the historical identities of the Gothic. He lives in the small eastern-Mediterranean town of Famagusta.

Paal Fagerheim is an assistant professor at Nesna University College, Norway and teaches popular music, world music, jazz history and music and globalisation. He is currently studying for his PhD in musicology. Paal is conducting research on popular music, especially hip hop, from the northern regions of Norway. He has also for many years been an active musician.

Tristan Fidler is a graduate from the University of Western Australia and is currently working there on his PhD thesis analyzing music video directors with reference to auteur theory, specifically focusing on Spike Jonze, Michel Gondry and Chris Cunningham.

David Hanner studied piano in Germany with Erich Appel and with Sebastian Benda in Graz, Austria and composition with Andrzej Dobrowolski, Jounghi Pagh-Paan, and Beat Furrer at the University of Music and Dramatic Arts in Graz, where he graduated in 1999. In master classes for piano, as well as chamber music and composition, he worked with Rudolph Kehrer in Moscow, the Franz Schubert Quartet in Vienna and Michael Jarrell in Geneva. David has received a number of awards for composition. He has worked as a freelance composer, held the position of Composer in Residence in Stift St. Lambrecht, Austria, and taught composition in Northern Cyprus and Hawaii. David Hanner's compositions have been performed by such well known ensembles as Szene Instrumental, Contrastrio, Klangforum Wien, the Ensemble Adventure, the Ensemble Sur Plus. David's work has also been performed at international festivals for contemporary music, such as the International Music Festival in Opatija, Wiener Hoergaenge, the Musik Bludenz, and June in Buffalo.

Dafydd Jones works in the field of the avant-garde and the neo-avant-garde, with particular departures from Dada, developing his address from philosophical and political bases. He has published within the *Crisis and the Arts: The History of Dada* series (2003), and edited the volume *Dada Culture: Critical Texts on the Avant-Garde* (2006); he was part of the Avant-Garde Project at the universities of Edinburgh and Glasgow, which closed with publication of *Neo-Avant-Garde* (edited by David Hopkins, 2006). Having completed doctoral research at the Centre for Critical and Cultural Theory at Cardiff University, he now lectures in contemporary art practice and theory at Cardiff, and is Editor of the University of Wales Press.

John MacKay, currently a resident of Western Massachusetts, USA, is a Canadian born pianist and scholar of 20th century and contemporary music. He is co-editor of *ex tempore,* an international review journal of musical analysis and has taught at a wide variety of schools in Canada, the USA, Portugal and Turkish North Cyprus. John has published several articles on Robert Erickson and, together with Erickson, he is co-author of *Music of Many Means: Sketches and Essays on the Music of Robert Erickson.* He enjoys cycling and travel.

Vincent Meelberg is Assistant Professor of Cultural Studies at Radboud University Nijmegen, the Netherlands. He studied double bass and music theory at the Rotterdam Conservatory, and received his MA in musicology and philosophy from Utrecht University. In 2006, he completed his PhD dissertation on the relation between narrativity and contemporary music from Leiden University, Department of Literary Studies. He is author of *New Sounds, New Stories: Narrativity in Contemporary Music.* Besides his academic activities, Vincent is a composer and remains active as a double bassist in several jazz groups.

Rodney Sharkey teaches literature at Cornell University, Doha campus. He has taught at Trinity College Dublin, Dublin City University, the University of Limerick and Eastern Mediterranean University in Cyprus. His specialised fields of interest are in Anglo-Irish literature, critical theory, performance dynamics and popular culture. He publishes regularly in journals such as *Modern Culture Reviews, Journal of Beckett Studies, Perspectives on Evil and Human Wickedness* and *Reconstruction.* Rodney Sharkey also produces and directs theatrical and musical events such as "Hair" (2001), "Catastrophe" (2002), "Glengarry Glen Ross" (2004) and "Baggage" (2005). He was the curator and director of the hugely successful Inscriptions in the Sand conference and arts festival, which became an annual event in Cyprus between 2002-2005.

John Wall has taught at universities in New Zealand, Ireland and Greece. He has published a number of articles on the relation between language and the body in the work of Samuel Beckett. Currently he is researching the concept of the "corporeal imagination", linking ontological explorations of the "productive" imagination with notions of embodied space, time and language. He is also editor of the forthcoming *Space of Mediations: Real Virtual Territories.* John Wall teaches literature at the Eastern Mediterranean University, Cyprus

INDEX